About the author

Angela Elwood is a keen photographer with a love of travel. After her twins grew up and left home, she embarked on a year of solo travel through South East Asia. She has enjoyed success in small business management and ownership, and currently shares ownership of a photographic business in Cardiff. She currently teaches English in a rural part of Thailand, returning home to the UK during Thai school holidays to catch up with family, friends and business. Find out more by visiting her at www.ayearinflipflops.co.uk on her page on Facebook or Instagram.

A YEAR IN FLIP-FLOPS

Sam,

be inspired!

Kind regards.

Angela Arnold. 21.10.17.

Angela Elwood

A YEAR IN FLIP-FLOPS

Vanguard Press

A CIP catalogue record for this title is
available from the British Library.

ISBN 978 1 784652 33 3

*Vanguard Press is an imprint of
Pegasus Elliot MacKenzie Publishers Ltd.*
www.pegasuspublishers.com

First Published in 2017

**Vanguard Press
Sheraton House Castle Park
Cambridge England**

Printed & Bound in Great Britain

Dedication

For Mum. You were only concerned about the risk I was taking. Even though you are gone now I sincerely hope that you are aware that I achieved my dream safely and that I am a better person for having done so.

Acknowledgements

Sincere thanks to my proof-readers who read emailed chapters as I wrote them up. Thank you for your encouragement – Mal Elwood, Gary Bullivant, Brian Baldock, Patti Davies, Dean Cark and Penny Jones.

Contents

Childhood Dreams

'Whether you think you can or whether you think you can't,
you're right.' Henry Ford

Many people have asked where and when did the idea to travel arise from. Good question! I believe the desire has always been there.

I remember an occasion, living in Banstead, in a cramped, top floor flat, sharing a bedroom with a brother and a step-brother, waking one morning clear in my intention to leave, to travel, to see the world. I was probably six at the time, so that wasn't really the right time to embark on a major journey alone. However, I remember getting out of bed; it was early, everyone was sleeping, my mum and my step-dad were asleep in the next room.

I woke my younger brother and insisted that he came with me to see the world, far horizons; we were going to travel. Being the big bossy sister that apparently I always was, and I guess still am, I loaded him with everything I thought we needed for the journey. Always a thoughtful child, I cut the butter, soap and loaf of bread in half, leaving half for my sleeping family. I rolled these provisions in a quilt and tied it to my brother's back. I carried a pair of sparkly, plastic kitten-healed flip-flops. Funny that! I can still see them hanging from the end of my hand as I packed him into the lift and walked down the stairs myself, I didn't trust the lift! After a visit to the local newsagent to buy sweets for the journey, using his pocket money of course, we were ready for adventure and off we went. Being an observant child I knew the direction to the coast and headed off on the main road toward Brighton. We were making great progress until my mum picked us up and boy, oh boy, did I cop it…

The intention to travel was always what I wanted to do before life kicked in, time and resources not available, timing inconvenient, never the right time for family and work commitments.

But the desire never left me, I was always fascinated by people who travelled, or who had lived overseas. I spent my time dreaming of boarding trains, boats, planes, anything. One of my favourite childhood book and film was *The Incredible Journey* by Sheila Burnford.

Well eventually the girl grew up, got married, got older, raised the kids, they left home and so she also left herself. The dreamed of journey could begin at last.

A Simple Stirring Of An Idea – Was This Possible?

I found myself, after many years bringing the kids up on my own and being single, faced with a choice. What next? What happens now? Both kids would be gone within the next year. I struggled, initially with panic, fear, life passing me by, was this it for me? Should I retire? I had felt invisible as a middle-aged woman, being able to pass by in the street or the park unnoticed. I had weathered years of long hours in retail, marriage, infertility, adoption and divorce. I had had to be so strong to raise our twins, manage the house and business, then deal with hormonal teenagers.

The school years had been difficult to navigate, for a variety of reasons. I can remember sitting up in bed on their eighteenth birthday and the first thought was, "We've made it!", when really what I probably meant was, "I've made it!". The years had been difficult. I had managed to muddle through with the help of close family members and a few close friends. I often found myself in Waterstones Bookshop perusing the Self Help section in search of something uplifting, something to sustain me.

I got involved with goal setting and life changing courses on-line, anything to keep myself going. When the children were smaller I had studied part time degree courses and had achieved an education up to Masters level. I found it difficult to discern where I was in life and was desperate to claw my way out of despair. I had, at times, felt like I was sinking and I fought hard against this feeling. I struggled with joining other parent groups at the pool, play area or school gate. I did not seem to fit in with the in-crowd. I was the mother with the child that was naughty or bit!

I took the decision to take a year off; a complete year away from everything and everybody. Was I mad? Could I do this? I had a good business, lovely house, excellent social life and a wide circle of friends. I travelled, took holidays, had interests, a good family, but, something was missing, I was feeling incomplete. I had to try to follow this crazy notion. My biggest fear was of getting lost. I had to believe that everything would be okay, I wouldn't get lost and even if I did I decided that I would stop, breathe, have a coffee, I could not give in to the fear. I wouldn't have tried if I had given in to fear or hesitated, I knew that. I would try. If everything went wrong or I was sick I was only a day away from home. There were few reasons to leave but more reasons to go, I had to at least try.

Preparing To Leave

I had been thinking about travelling for a while. I guess I was also influenced by some of the literature I had recently read, such as the well known and probably best loved *Eat, Pray, Love* by Elizabeth Gilbert. A couple of other favourite texts of mine which helped me were *Wild*, written by Cheryl Strayed and *Feel The Fear And Do It Anyway* written by Susan Jeffers. I had been feeling restless for a while, wondering what to do next. My son was applying to join the RAF and his twin had left several months previously. Suddenly I would be home alone in a large house, what was I do? What was the next step? Rent? Move? Take in lodgers?

Then I was sitting in my garden talking to a neighbour about the UK and how unhappy we were as a nation. She had recently moved to Canada with her family. It was a good conversation about the present state of the nation from an outside observer. As soon as she left I knew exactly what I wanted to do more than anything, I was going to take a Gap Year. Funnily, I knew exactly where I wanted to go – South East Asia and end up in Australia before returning home twelve months later.

This was nine months before the start of my trip. I had planned to depart at the end of the financial year for the business, once all the accounts had been filed and bills paid. The date was set for 20 April 2015. This was not an impulsive decision, this was something that had slowly simmered on the back boiler, so to speak, and now I needed time to make sure it would happen.

I guess one of the questions I would have reading a book such as this is how did I finance my trip? The house rental paid for the mortgage. I was lucky to benefit from a fair divorce settlement and was granted the rental payments of three flats above the business. I dropped my salary to half and only drew it couple of times during the year. Once the flights, medical, visas, passport and volunteer projects were paid for, I simply needed enough for accommodation, food and transport. All of these can be so cheap in Asia. It depends on where you want to stay, what you want to eat and how you want to travel. To give you an example of each, a hostel room can cost a little as $5 a night, with bathroom and towel, a meal on the street less than £1 and the entire journey from Saigon, south Vietnam to Hue further up north cost $35.

I wanted life to carry on at home without me, although I hoped I'd be missed in some way! I bought a journal suitable for planning. I love notebooks so, like any other book I bought, this book had to be right. The hunt for it was all part of the pleasure. I found it and subdivided it into sections – family and personal, the business and the trip itself. In the personal section I planned the rental of my house and the management of the properties, who would have the cats, who would be around for the kids, selling my car. The business section covered lists of things that needed to be done to ensure adequate staff cover, payment of regular bills, processing payroll and management of the accounts.. In the trip section of the notebook I made lists of things I needed to do before leaving, for example: get any jabs needed, malaria protection, research and plan routes, apply for any visas required.

Gradually everything I wished for began to happen. I had made my decision and all the doors were opening. I had given myself enough time to prepare thoroughly and plan well. This was essential as I was stepping out of my life for a year. As I previously said, I wanted it to work, not only for me but for those around me.

Firstly, I had tell people, and tell people in a particular order as there are some that I wanted to tell myself and not for them to hear second-hand. Close friends, work colleagues and family came first. Without exception everyone was pleased for me. I was amazed by their reaction, how brave everyone thought I was. I felt humbled by the number of people who followed my journey remotely, delighting in and commenting on the images I put up on Facebook or Instagram. I guess there are more who would literally join me, or do something similar, if the opportunity presented itself.

The only person who was negative about my trip was my mum who just looked at me, expressed surprise and questioned my likeness to anyone in the family. She was concerned that I would be murdered on a beach somewhere. To her the world appeared dangerous and not to be trusted. In her eyes for me to take this trip was reckless and, quite frankly, ridiculous. Poor Mum was not well at the time, had not been well for many years. She passed away in the January before I left in the April. She never got to worry about me but the regret is that I will never get to share my experience with her, reassure her of my safety and ability to look after myself, or send her cards which I know she would have enjoyed.

The preparation continued. I read guidebooks and spent a happy week in Turkey making endless lists of things I would need. And do you know I didn't need half of the recommended items! Think carefully, if you plan to do this; everything you take you have to carry. I particularly enjoyed *High Heels and a Head Torch* by Chelsea Duke, a book I found both encouraging and moving. I put up maps on my kitchen wall to look at each day and to become familiar with them. I began to find the task of mapping an exact route arduous and recognized a feeling of panic as I saw the 365 days stretch out before me. I visited Stanfords bookshop in Covent Garden on three occasions to get inspiration and more guidebooks, each time standing in front of the shelves of SE Asia and being moved to tears. Was I really doing this? Was it possible? Time and time again I asked myself what would happen if I got lost or stuck somewhere, became confused or frightened?

The size of the venture began to overwhelm me at the early stages until a very close and wise friend suggested that I consider the whole time as being broken down into sections of two weeks, planning for two weeks at a time only and then moving on. This made a great deal of sense and provided much needed reassurance. I didn't have to meticulously plan each day, each stretch of travel, every place to stay but rather loosely decide the route for the year. This approach enabled me to organize the visas that were needed to be applied for before I left the UK. Additionally, I decided to renew my passport as I would need space to put all the stamps and visa stickers for each country. Thank goodness I did, my new passport is now full as some countries have a large sticker that requires a full page. The internet provided information about visa requirements; most were available on entry but I wanted to check as I was planning to enter countries overland and not through airports.

An essential part of the preparation was to take action to safeguard my health against foreign germs and infections I could pick up on my trip. I booked in to see the nurse at my GP surgery and together we planned all the injections I would need by looking at my intended route. I had to use the travel clinic to get Japanese Encephalitis vaccine and also protection against rabies.

Protection against rabies is vitally important as the timing of getting treatment after a bite or scratch from any mammal is paramount. By having the injection I was allowing more time to get to a hospital, if the worse happened, and I would not need a blood transfusion, something not recommended as blood that side of the world is not as thoroughly scanned as it is in the UK. Because of this I packed my own needles.

Another issue was protection against malaria, how long to take the tablets, in what countries to take the tablets and which tablet to take. This protection all added up to several hundreds of pounds but I felt it was important for me to take care of known risks to my health. In addition, I purchased an insurance policy that would cover any event overseas for a year, including being transported back in a bag or on a drip! Joking aside, all of these were necessary preparations.

Christmas was as always the event that needed to be endured and got past. I knew that the time was passing but as soon as Christmas and New Year were over, like a train on the tracks, the momentum would carry me hurtling toward my leaving date.. I was right. The time did fly with extreme speed, the time was fast approaching when it would be the moment to leave, all the plans and preparations were happening. And yet there was still a sense of unreality or maybe disbelief, even though I had made the decision to go and was preparing to leave. I took a month away from the business in January, the quietest time. This enabled me to assess a new rota and staff levels; also declutter the house and clear rooms ready for renting it.

The funniest part of this being in the house, clearing away or recycling items no longer required, was the clearing out of my son's bedroom. His domain remained stacked to the ceiling with his belongings and, quite frankly, rubbish. I left him to it. He is a last minute operator who needs a firm but short deadline. He was astonished to find that despite the fact that he was leaving home too, and that his room would be rented along with the rest of the house, his bedroom would not remain his territory. He really thought that his room would stay the same, just as he left it, waiting for his return. On the last evening before vacating the house his room was finally cleared and his possessions safely stored in the attic.

I had planned to leave our house two weeks before leaving the country. This was a good plan. The emotional task of leaving my home was heart-wrenching and I was glad to retreat to the home of a family member rather than be sitting on a train to the airport, upset, crying and worrying if I was doing the right thing, full of regret rather than anticipation. This was another aspect of the planning which had gone well. A fortnight later I was free to make my exit. I had made a careful list of what needed to be done and gradually worked my way through it to successfully free myself for my trip. The journal, separated into sections – home/family, business and trip – had done its job. I was ready.

The final two weeks were taken up with farewells to friends and family. I made sure I spent time with everyone, all my various social and friend groups. It soon became clear that I needed to organise an event as a final farewell as everyone expressed a desire to meet up and do something before I left, but time was passing and everyone was busy with their own lives. One of my close friends organised an afternoon tea, I made arrangements to meet most of my friends, in their groups or individually, and I arranged a Sunday lunch at a nearby pub. All these occasions meant so much to me and I felt proper farewells had been said. My best friend and I made sure we enjoyed a Saturday night out and sup our final Sunday afternoon bottle of red in our favourite local wine bar.

I boarded the train from Cardiff Central to Heathrow. I did not wish to have any 'airport farewells' as these can be traumatic and upsetting. I wanted to leave and leave quietly. Time to reflect on what I was embarking on as I sat on the train to London. I arrived in Heathrow after changing trains in Paddington. I could hardly walk as my backpack was so heavy! Before checking in I went through the contents and took out a load of items I thought I wouldn't need, like a coat, umbrella, several duplicated plugs and chargers. I left them in sight of a bin in the hope that someone who needed them would pick them up. I boarded the plane to Bangkok, a straight through flight, and looked out of the window at a grey day in the UK.

It was 20 April 2015. I was ready to go, I would be returning one year from now if everything went to plan. I had spent the last couple of weeks shedding the odd tear as I said my farewells. As I sat on the plane waiting for it to take off I felt nothing but an overwhelming sense of the start of an adventure.

I landed eleven hours later in a sweltering Bangkok. I walked through the airport to collect my backpack, purchase a local sim card for my phone and take a taxi in to the city centre to stay the first three nights in a decent, mid range hotel. This hotel had a wonderful sky bar. I sat, glass of white wine in front of me and looked out at the afternoon Bangkok skyline. It was hot and bright, noisy from traffic and trains. I had arrived... I sat and thought about what I had done to get this far.

I spent three days in Bangkok at the beginning, learning how to get around the city by BTS train and tuk tuk. I made the mistake of looking like a novice traveller, map in hand as I walked, and got into a tuk tuk suggested by a 'helpful' man, helping me find my way around. He took me to some sites but on the way we had to pop into some tailors for a short visit. The tailors pay the drivers in litres of fuel for each customer that was brought to their workshops. The 'tour' was taking a while and I began to get worried. I received a fake call on my phone and pretended that my friends had arrived back at our hotel and were looking for me.

I booked another trip to see a train drive through a market just outside Bangkok and visit the floating markets. The floating markets were interesting but touristy. The train was an amazing sight as it goes through the market twice daily, each time the market traders move back and fold away tarpaulins to make room for it to go past. After enjoying Bangkok I met my

Cambodian guide, by the main train station although we were taking a minibus from close by. He was going to kick-start my entire trip by taking me on a tour of Cambodia. I had planned this before leaving the UK as I feared arriving in Asia and the I was ready to embark on my tour of Cambodia, a country I was fascinated by and longing to see.

I was ready to go. *'Life is a journey, not a destination.'* Ralph Waldo Emerson

Cambodia

I arrived overland from Bangkok to Cambodia in a minibus. I was the only westerner on the bus. It made for interesting travel as we stopped off at service areas selling locally produced snacks of a variety of confection made from rice. Travelling by bus in Asia was cheap and convenient, certainly amusing, if a little uncomfortable at times. I learnt very quickly not to look out of the front window at the oncoming traffic. There are three lanes most of the time, whether the road is wide enough or not and the driver who was the bravest heads straight through the middle.

It was a wonderful way to spend the day looking out at the fields and countryside. I spent hours working at my crochet, just looking and learning from the world passing my bus window. I never understood the people who when travelling on the bus, closed the curtains and went to sleep. Travelling on buses was unexpectedly a very interesting, albeit slow way, to travel in SE Asia. They are bumpy and packed, but reliable and cheap. Beware – don't sit on the back seat, as I normally would love to do, as the roads are full of bumps. These are sped over at great speed sending the passengers at the back of the bus off their seats and flying!

This happened on every bridge, as each one has a bump at the start and at the end. The buses and cars using these roads were usually overloaded with passengers sitting on the roof or hanging off the back of the tailgates. The boot would be dropped down to provide another set of seats. The cities, as they refer to them, were very poor and ramshackle.

Be prepared to share your seat with a chicken or a bucket of fish going to market, as well as any number of people sitting on the same seat as you. But the people are friendly and can be entertaining, and even though the journey could be perilous, they all appeared to have their own supply of sick bags at the ready. The Cambodian countryside was mile after mile of rice fields, water buffalo, fruit fields, acres of reddish brown soil punctuated by roadside shacks. The roads are straight, but made of red dust.

Toilets, like buses, are also worth a cautionary note. They are both familiar and unfamiliar everyday things. Some are squat, with tiny doors and extremely slippery floors, others mere holes in the floor, all especially hazardous if wearing soft rubber flip-flops. I always had a pack in my handbag containing toilet paper and handwash as the availability of both of these was totally unreliable. I replenished my supply from hotels or hostels.

The border at Poipet was extremely busy, men crossing over to find work, farmers and traders loaded to the hilt with their produce. It was an amazing sight, something I would have missed coming in by plane but now thankfully had witnessed first-hand. My biggest fears had been crossing such borders by myself, finding buses, getting lost; all these worrying factors. To help me over initial hurdles and prevent me from flying home on the next plane to Heathrow, I engaged a Cambodian guide who personally showed me the heart of his country. He guided me through practical things like how to get bus tickets, how to travel with the locals and enjoy the experience of his country away from the beaten track.

This was perfect. I was able to relax and satisfy my inquisitive mind by asking questions about the war and what happened afterwards. He, like most other Cambodians, had lost family members in the genocide that had taken place under the Khmer Rouge in Cambodia during the 1970s. He had also been a monk for a period in his life. Even the monks had been disrobed during the time of conflict and put to work or, worse still, slaughtered just like everyone else.

I had the pleasure of staying at the home of my guide's family. It was a beautiful, simple Khmer household, growing fruit and vegetables, a pond for fish, chickens in the backyard, home grown herbs and home cooking. Everyone helps prepare the food for the extended family that lives within the household. There was great respect for the mother from all members. They all ate together, sitting on the floor of their home, sharing food from communal serving bowls. Interestingly, little portions were taken and eaten at a time, unlike our habit of eating a meal served on individual plates. There was rice wine infused with tarantulas available too! The kitchen was outside the main home; very basic, an open fire used for cooking.

Although the family were very poor in material ways I loved the simple freedom of their natural surroundings and the way the family lived together. The children enjoyed the freedom of open fields to run through, mud to wade in, stone throwing games and lakes to swim in whilst catching fish for family meals. The simple pleasure of being free, even though that freedom was enjoyed in some of the most poverty stricken areas of Siem Reap, whilst less than a mile away were the high rise four star hotels of the visitors and tourists to Angkor Wat where they enjoyed complete opulence.

At the start of the war the Khmer Rouge had marched into Phnom Penh and ordered everybody to leave for three days as the Americans were about to bomb the city. The Americans had used Cambodia as a base to get to Vietnam where it was fighting the Communist northern Vietcong. On their return to the city everyone was told to report to the army command and provide information on family status. The army authority rounded anyone up with a profession, took these families to 're-education' centres, which were in fact holding prisons, before being taken for slaughter. Whole families were killed and flung into pits to be buried, babies smashed against trees before they too joined their families in the pits.

This was a horrible reign of terror lasting just over two years. It was important to me to know this history, but not to dwell on it, as it explained who the people are today. It provided an insight in to the way the people operated, they seemed to forgive but not forget; they moved on and rebuilt their lives. Everyone has been scarred and lost loved ones. Families fled and split up during the terror in an effort to save each other. At the end of the war it became impossible to relocate people or bury the remains of loved ones as it was impossible to find them or identify them. Many tried to flee the country. Looking around at the people it was obvious to me that there was almost a missing generation, lots of young and old, but not so many middle-aged.

Cambodia has been badly affected by the murders of nearly half a population, three million people were killed, out of a total population of seven million, by the Khmer Rouge. I felt shocked that this had taken place during my lifetime, probably during my school days when I relentlessly stared out of the window during lessons. The world didn't know until much later. The Khmer Rouge was master minded and led by a man named Pol Pot, not his real name but rather a political one being a shortened version of 'political potential'.

He was influenced by communism during a visit to Yugoslavia when he was being educated in France. Along with a few other like-minded young men and one woman excessive control was applied to manipulate the people of Cambodia. They feared the middle class, the educated and skilled, as they were most likely to be the ones who caused most objection and therefore trouble.

I was delighted with the company of my guide. From our conversations I was able to gain such an insight into the background and people. The visit to the city of Angkor, which included the very famous Angkor Wat, was fascinating. It took three days to get around the entire city. I was able to watch the sunrise over Angkor Wat and then explore the other temples on foot, entering through the jungle to Angkor Thorn to be enthralled by the ancient ruins being dwarfed by tree roots but otherwise more or less totally undisturbed. The site has beautiful relief murals depicting beliefs and life from the time of the Angkor people. It was possible to see the war damage of bullet holes, some with bullets still remaining in, on the walls of the ancient monument.

Together we explored rural areas on push-bikes and on the back of his motorbike. I cycled across a half mile long bamboo bridge, sharing the narrow carriageway with motorbikes and small vehicles, hard on the knees and as well as the nerves. I was rewarded at the end of this particular experience with diving straight into the Mekong River, fully clothed. This was the sort of added experience of Cambodia I gained from being led by my guide, Bun.

The Mekong River flows through Cambodia. It is a source of food and part of everyday life. The people live in it, on it, wash themselves in the water and do their laundry in it and feed from it. This natural source is under threat from China and Laos who are damming the river at its source higher up. Tonlé Sap is a lake that is fed annually by the Mekong, refreshing its fish stock and irrigating the land. The people who dwell on the lake live in houses on stilts and floating on bamboo. Every year the entire village is removed house by house, a communal effort to survive the rising tide of the lake. This lifestyle, and others in Cambodia, will be changed forever by the dams.

It was during the travel down through Cambodia that I had my first experience of becoming lost. This was something I had dreaded and quite honestly it was my own fault. I decided to take a tuk tuk into the town centre to eat in the evening and then walk back to my hotel. I should have done it the other way round, walked in, tuk tuk home. I wandered back, fully confident I had remembered the way. I walked and walked. It got darker and darker. I started to retrace my footsteps when I realized I had gone wrong. At one point there was a pack of dogs following me, not quite menacing but certainly not friendly. I had to turn around to them repeatedly and click my finger, saying firmly "stay". I'm sure the language was lost on them but the tone of my voice was unwavering, which certainly wasn't how I felt inside!

There were people sat around in groups drinking and playing cards, locals not tourists. I came across two tuk tuk drivers and asked for help, they simply laughed at me so I walked on. I came across another driver, older, to whom I showed my map and pointed where I wanted to go. I offered a fare of two dollars, a fortune to them, if he got me back to my hotel. It took less than two minutes to get back, I was one street away. He shrugged and I simply said he had earned the fare as he had got me out of a pickle. Lesson of the day was to make sure I know where I am going or to take a ride back.

Generally, the Cambodians are a very proud and generous people, although in many cases extremely poor. I enjoyed two home stays during my time there. They are hard working, rising early each day to go to the market to sell or purchase food to feed their families. It took me a while to learn to appreciate the sheer hard life some of these people lived, growing their crops, going to market, preparing food from basic ingredients and all the other daily tasks.

Their homes are built on stilts due to the rainy season when the land floods, irrigating the rice crops. They have little furniture, eat sitting on the floor together and sleep either on the floor or a pallet. Extended families live together. I was impressed by the society I witnessed here. Women were genuinely respected, especially the mother. Everyone pulled together to make the life for the family work. Some families have to travel to work if there is none around and would leave their children with other family members.

The children had a simple freedom. They swam in the rivers and lakes, fished and played; such blissful freedom, but very poor. I witnessed children playing scratch games, the game of jacks using stones, and flip-flops were used for a game of bowling. They get up early and take themselves to school, sharing bikes with their siblings and friends.

I visited the floating villages that dwell on the Tonlé Sap. The houses were made of wood and floated on tyres in the waters of the lake. The lake is tidal so each year the village is moved up and down the lake as the water ebbs and flows. The fish stocks are replaced during this time. The village moves together, all of the houses being towed by the joined forces of the village people. Everything was on the lake that they require, shops, schools, etc. A whole village floating and living off Tonlé Sap lake. An incredible way of life.

I visited the killing fields in Phnom Pehn. These were particularly disturbing and the experience was even more poignant knowing that these were just an example of the many killing fields all over Cambodia. There were skulls piled high in a central memorial to the dead. There were photographs of each person that had been brought in for 'correction' and items of clothing displayed in cabinets. A tree had ribbons tied to it to remember the babies that had been executed by having their skulls bashed upon it. It was a disturbing memorial. I found nothing but silence as I walked around. There were bits of bones coming up through the paths where I walked. So many have yet to be discovered and laid to rest. It was a horrible monument to a disturbing event in their history. I could not even take a photograph, yet I noticed a group of tourists taking 'selfies'. The visit to the killing fields was followed by a visit to one of the schools that had been used as a prison. Again there were photographs of the people taken there and horrific evidence remaining on the walls and floors of the atrocities they had suffered at the hands of the Khmer Rouge. These two places were difficult to visit one after the other but I felt in some way I had paid respect to those who had died here.

After travelling right the way down through the Cambodian countryside by bus I took a break by the beach, exploring the islands and snorkelling in clear waters. Here I encountered many young backpackers from Europe and America, enjoying the relative cheapness and freedom of Cambodian life. Beer and accommodation were cheap here, beach life easy.

Like most of their Asian cousins the Cambodians eat anything. I was determined to try anything offered to me. I ate at roadside food shacks, which seemed very safe as it was where the locals ate each day and congregate. I tried tarantula, crickets, tree ants, eggs with a foetus still inside, sticky rice in banana leaf and other local homemade snacks. I ate locally wherever possible and did not suffer one bout of food poisoning or other outcomes!

Tourism will provide this country with the influx of money needed to support the coming generations. However, for tourism to be successful, the people need to speak English to get good jobs and make a better future. I spent three weeks with a project teaching English in a school in Takeo district. This was a poor, farming area, extremely rural and for me was a brilliant experience. It was uncomfortable and dirty. I left the company of my guide to board a tuk tuk with a driver who had no English or understanding or where I was going. He took me first to an orphanage and then after some discussion to the project at Hope. As I sat travelling through rural farming fields in the open tuk tuk I felt quite tearful and frightened of where I was going and what was going to happen next. I caught myself feeling like this and changed my thinking to my positive thoughts. Everything would be okay. I arrived finally at the project and was greeted by the English supervisor who showed me around. I needn't have worried.

The conditions, for the volunteers, were very basic. However, I never regretted being there, nor wanted to go home. I can remember lying in a hard bunk bed, a very noisy but useless fan going round in the ceiling and thinking about my comfortable house and bed at home but not wishing to be there. The kids ranged from the age of four to late teens. They were so rewarding and entertaining, giving so much more to me than I could ever offer them. I still carry the letter the older girls wrote to me asking me to return. 'Pretty teacher, good teacher, you come back in September.' I had no regrets. I was working with other volunteers from the UK, much younger than me, and enjoyed their company very much. On the weekends we would take the opportunity to go and stay at places such as Sihanoukville, Kampot and Phnom Penh. This was where I learnt that hostels are much better than described in the guide books, very comfortable, chilled, comfy-clean beds, basic bathrooms, but good food and pools – all for five dollars a night! This was really the time when I learnt that I could share food, get squashed in minibuses and squeeze in a bed with another girl to get the five dollar charge down to two and half dollars! Great for the budget but I promised myself a decent hotel when I finished the project and reached Saigon in Vietnam, my new destination.

.

Vietnam

Saigon – Mekong Delta – Muine – Dalat – Na Trang – Hoi An – Hue – Ha Noi – Halong Bay – Sapa – Ha Noi

Vietnam was completely different to Cambodia. Same killing heat, causing oppressive sweating, but a different vibe. How can simply stepping over a border make such a difference?

The difference I perceived was in history and the people. The Chinese ruled Vietnam for a thousand years. Although the Chinese were oppressive and demanding rulers the Vietnamese gained a great deal from the Chinese culture, for example, rice cultivation and water irrigation. Also, looking at the palaces and temples, there was evidence of this long rule. Any official documents had to be written in Chinese as the local language was only a spoken language until it was formalised by the French in 1910. Interestingly, Vietnamese was a tonal language but has a Latin based alphabet.

The French colonised Vietnam in 1883 until 1954. They were tough and tyrannical rulers but, as I said before, left their mark on the country, not only in the formalization of the language but also leaving some beautiful colonial buildings behind, especially in Hanoi and Saigon.

After the Geneva Accords of 1954 Vietnam was divided into north and south. The North being under the influence of its large neighbour China and a more communist regime, whereas the South sided with America against communism. A huge, conveniently placed mountain pass provided a clear division between the two. For thirty-one years, 1953-85, the North fought the South in a pointless, bloody war. The South was supported by America and the neighbouring countries, supplied arms and troops; the war was bigger than just North versus South Vietnam.

Cu Chi is a small province in the south that supported the north. It was here that guerilla warfare took place, farmer by day but soldier by night; no one could trust anyone else, there was an atmosphere of fear. The guerillas, hiding in tunnels, set traps for the American troops close to their main base. Their missions did not result in much killing but the psychological threat was great.

The sad thing being that these people, although they supported communism, had no idea how badly their northern neighbours lived under such hard communist rule. The people of the north were starving and living under extremely poor conditions.

The war went on until a conference was called in France with the Americans, Vietnamese, French and Vietcong (northerners) to end the war in 1973. The Vietcong refused to attend. America bombed Hanoi for twelve days until they too finally agreed to attend. Eventually a ceasefire strategy was put together. America kept to their agreement and went home but the northern Vietcong continued to push through southern Vietnam until ultimately they captured Saigon in April 1975, thus winning the war. Vietnam ceased to be a divided country and the collapse of the Soviet Union in the 1990s, loosening the hold of communism, has encouraged foreign investment.

That was a very vague outline of the history of this fascinating country. However, it was vital to have an idea of the background as it provided an insight into the people they are today. This was one hard working, successful nation. I witnessed extraordinary enterprise, from early morning coffee being available from flasks on plastic chairs outside train stations to impromptu parking lots on market days for the thousands of bikes in the city centres. It felt vibrant, busy and on the way up, busily constructing new and beautiful accommodation to satisfy a booming tourism industry.

After the hostels and project in Cambodia I promised myself a decent hotel in Saigon. It was possible to balance the budget in this way. Accommodation had been cheap in Cambodia, now time for a spoil. I arrived in Saigon, incidentally still called Saigon by the locals but renamed as part of the reunification to HCMC (Ho Chi Minh City), after having travelled over the border from Phnom Penh on a comfortable tourist bus with free wifi.

Cautionary note – always, always find out the rate of exchange before arriving in another country. I made the mistake of not knowing the value of the Vietnamese Dong and attempting to take money from an ATM to pay for a taxi without a clue on how much to withdraw. I ended up turning to the queue behind me for help. Additionally, the taxi driver overcharged me, which was frankly as much as I deserved for being so clueless. I learnt quickly to read the guidebook I had brought with me and, with some more thorough research, be a bit more savvy. But like life, some lessons are learnt too late or as you bumble along.

Although Vietnam was now a united country, north and south, there still appeared to be a division in the thinking and attitude of the people. Wars had taken their toll but it appeared that the most hatred and certainly the most remembered, was the intervention of the USA. Propaganda told of the wrongs of the Americans, usually without any reference to the part the Vietcong, the North Vietnamese, played.

Interestingly, in one day I heard two completely different views, one from a taxi driver who was convinced Americans still only come to Vietnam nowadays to kill its people. He made it sound like a cruel sport. The other was a southern guide who took me to see the Cu Chi tunnels. This guide gave information on both sides, a very balanced viewpoint, which, for me, was only destroyed later when I visited the museum of war remnants and saw the photographic evidence of the appalling Agent Orange, the chemical sprayed throughout Vietnam by the Americans to destroy the foliage and eliminate the places for the Vietcong to hide. From what I could surmise, it really was a messy, ugly, pointless war. The effects of Agent Orange had consequences for the ordinary people of Vietnam from one generation to the next.

The first thing that hit me about Saigon, or in fact any city in Vietnam, was the traffic. The motorbikes. There are literally thousands of them. Whole families ride together on a single bike, anything and everything is carried, dead or alive, on a bike. Cars are so expensive and definitely in the minority, while the bikes are easy and cheap.

On arrival I was pinned to one side of the road by my fear of attempting to cross to the other side. It became necessary to overcome this fear of crossing the road or submit to seeing

Saigon from one side of the road only. I started to shadow anyone who seemed to know what they were doing, attaching myself very closely to them as they crossed to the other side of the road. Although there were lights and crossings these seemed to be totally ignored by the bikes.

At one time, quite late at night, I was dithering on the road trying to summon the courage to make my way across. I was frustrated as the previous night I had had to take a taxi to a hotel that I could see from where I was pinned due to this understandable but useless fear of crossing the road. I was standing waiting to cross and a man appeared at my side, took my hand and led me across two busy junctions. I am ashamed to report that I thought he was going to take me somewhere I did not want to go or ask for money. He did neither. Safely on the other side, he did a slight bow and walked briskly away, turning to wave before disappearing. I will forever consider him to be my 'crossing angel'. I was greatly moved by his gesture.

This was not the first or last time I experienced help from unknown strangers, providing for me exactly what I needed when I was lost or simply missing connection with others. The same happened in Hanoi, the other end of my Vietnam travels. As I struggled again crossing roads in busy traffic, someone took my by the elbow and guided me across. Needless to say, after a time I worked out the way to cross a busy road was to move step by step into the spaces between the bikes until reaching the other side. The bikes go round pedestrians, the real danger was the buses and lorries. But learning to cross the road safely out in Asia meant I could relax and simply enjoy exploring.

It is difficult to describe my experience in Vietnam without sounding like the Lonely Planet Guide. My intention with writing about this experience was not to describe each place but Vietnam was so different at each stop. From wide expanses of sand, to ancient seaports, busy cities, ancient tombs and Cham sites, it has something different at every stop from north to south. The travel was easy to organize and I purchased a ticket that took me from Saigon to Hue by bus and then on from Hue by train to Hanoi. It cost less for the bus, thirty-five dollars all the way including a night bus then the one overnight train, which was sixty dollars. But otherwise cheap travel compared to our prices in the UK. The buses were comfortable and clean, also the fare included being picked up from the hostel or hotel to get to the stop where the bus would leave. It was incredibly easy to do.

The very famous Halong Bay was outstandingly beautiful but spoilt by having so many tourists. I think my favourite experience will always be trekking in Sapa, staying and being guided by the hill tribe people. Yet, even here there had become a strong touristy feel to the trip. I travelled from Hanoi in an overnight sleeper train, arriving at the station before being driven in a mini bus to the heights of Sapa. The trekking experience was beautiful, a real thrill not to be missed but the terrain plays havoc on aging knees and out of condition thighs. It was incredibly taxing on the legs, the slopes were vertical and extremely slippery. I worried for the safety of my two doll-like guides, both carrying a baby in a basket on their backs.

I went with a small group of travellers who were great company. They were from Switzerland and The Netherlands. Aided by my tiny guides I scrambled up and down the steep, muddy slopes, enjoying the views of rice fields and hand built terraces. We passed children riding water buffalo and indigenous tribes in traditional costumes walking through the hills. The doll-like ladies walking with us had perfect English, which when asked how such perfect English had been learnt they said they had learnt from talking with tourists. I enjoyed their company very much. I took advantage of using a homestay and enjoyed an evening of rice wine and card games.

The village women who came to the village of Sapa were incredibly talented, very skilled in selling their wares, great company, following me around and waiting if I called in somewhere for a coffee. They stood outside the café as they were not made welcome by the café owners, I guess most tourists find them a nuisance. Without too much persuasion, I bought gifts from the ladies, insisting on the homemade variety rather than the packaged, cheap items obviously shipped in from China. I agreed only to buy from the guides in whose company I had managed to trek the twenty-one kilometers from the main village to the homestay. It was necessary to put a limit on how much to buy, they are extremely persuasive and it is difficult to turn them down. Like so many times in SE Asia I was reminded how hard the women have to work to manage family life and make money to live on.

This short account can not do justice to my time in Vietnam. On the coach trip in from Cambodia I had been concerned at how I would fare on my own. I need not have worried. I had loosely planned a route but had no specific details of where to stay or how to get from place to place. Vietnam has astounded me in its hard working attitude, frustrated me at times with its scams and hard selling women, but who can blame them? Here was a country getting on its feet and doing very well after a long and pointless war.

I left Vietnam wiser about solo travel. I found getting around incredibly cheap and easy. Buses are comfortable, sure some journeys can be very long but they are remarkably affordable. The trains can be a bit bewildering but once I had worked out how to read the ticket it was easy to go to the correct part of the platform to board the berth to which I had been assigned. It was easy!

I found people mostly friendly and helpful, and I had some extremely funny exchanges and gestured conversations despite no shared language, and especially with the women. The Vietnamese women are canny, inquisitive and forthcoming, especially the older ones who have an innate, natural beauty about them. Collectively I find them noisy! The locals have an endless ability to make money from any occasion. It was wise to be aware of this when holding onto the budget funds but I became aware of a growing respect and awe at their money-making skills. However, on the way to this appreciation I learnt the hard way in Hanoi. I had what could have been a very unpleasant experience with a man who mended my flip-flops. One of these flip-flops had a small rip but they were holding out, the only problem being the slipperiness of the soles in the wet streets. A man stopped me, pointed to my flip-flop, took it off my foot and mended the rip with superglue. He then resoled the shoe, making it non-slip. But this was only one shoe. I offered him money, but he demanded more, I gave in seeing the pointlessness of any argument but passed him my other shoe to be resoled as well.

The first man disappeared after I paid him, and the other sole was replaced by two other men who, in turn, both demanded more money. I refused this time, and after a very unpleasant exchange I walked away, with two non-slip, resoled flip-flops! I could have probably bought a new pair with the price of the repair but these were precious Aussie thongs that I bought on a previous trip to Australia.

Despite the unpleasantness of the exchange I had to marvel at the tenacity of their salesmanship and for spotting a tasty gap in the market. But the lesson here was never let anyone do anything for you without finding out how much!

I had found the people in Vietnam to be enterprising and hard-working. The women were amazing. Beautiful older ladies had a certain dignity about them, small, lovely features and extremely mobile. A visit to the Women's Museum in Ha Noi provided an insight into the lives of women through time in this war-troubled country. Women had worked in the home, brought up the families, made items of clothing and housewares and played an important role in the civil war. There was information about women whose husbands had become sick, injured or died and who had been forced to come into the cities, like Ha Noi to earn a living. They usually shared houses in the city for cheap rent and sold on the city streets, sending home money to provide for their families.

Life could be very hard in this part of the world. I sat one evening on a balcony overlooking a crowded market in the old part of Ha Noi. Below me pedestrians and riders squeezed through narrow streets. It was noisy and hot. I could see two women shouting on different corners and gesturing to all the bikes. I asked what they were shouting at the bikes. They were shouting, "Come in, bike, come in!" to show bikes a place to park. Each woman had set up a temporary car park and was collecting money for parking in the street by the markets. It was hilarious but what a great idea!

I left Vietnam feeling I had progressed even more as a solo traveller. I had worked out my route, ways to travel and places to stay. I found that the internet was a great resource for booking hostels and finding out something about them before arriving. I left the country feeling grateful for many small graces. I had made friends and had experienced many good times to add to the memory bank. I had enjoyed the company of strangers, some I would probably never hear from or see again, others remain friends via social net working sites.

It was rather an odd experience being collected from my hotel in Hanoi. A rider arrived on motorbike for three of us, plus luggage. He took our bags and told us to follow him to the pick up point for the overnight bus to Laos. It was really difficult trying to get through the busy, narrow streets and follow a bike rider among throng of others on bikes. I had not met my fellow travellers before this pick up but we soon bonded together in an effort to keep up with our luggage. We did take a wrong turning and had to retrace our footsteps. At the end of a short panic we located our bags on the back of a bike in the distance and ran in pursuit.

I fell in love with the country. I have described its people as having a great business acumen and the border guards were busily lining their own pockets by charging a dollar to stamp a passport. You don't argue with a dollar and I remember being amused by the pile of passports waiting for the stamp and the dollar bills being tossed in a drawer one after the other.

The fact that the border guards were swigging beer at seven in the morning only added to the absurdity of the whole experience and the fact that I had just got off an overnight bus bound for Laos after being sat at the border for four hours already, waiting for the border to open. It had been an uncomfortable wait as the engine had been switched off and so had the air con. However, we were first in line in the queue to cross the border... small mercies and all that came to mind.

I would urge anyone reading this to visit Vietnam and do it sooner rather than later. At the time of writing this book it was cheap to travel around it and cheap accommodation. There was a great deal of building going on, a surge in tourism, a new Rivera. Go before it loses some of its authentic, old charm and, undoubtedly, the prices go up! Or, worse still, the Russians beat you to it...

Laos

Vieniane – Luang Prabang – Two days on the Mekong travelling to Thailand

There was a time at the start of my Laos experience that I would have concurred with Greene on this view. After a twenty-four hour bus ride from Hanoi and a hilarious border crossing I arrived in an unremarkable Vientiane. The overnight bus had dropped us off outside the city centre and there were tuk tuk wagon like vehicles waiting to finish the journey. These looked like wagons that would be used to transport animals, hard, narrow bench seats, our bags were slung up on the roof above our heads. Vientiane takes time to appreciate, its chilled atmosphere and numerous temples I guess after an impressive Vietnam I was somewhat disappointed. But this was my judgment.

The best thing for me about this city was hiring a pushbike and following a cycle route of the city in the Lonely Planet guide, and also, a gem of a wine bar very close to my hotel. I enjoyed cheese and wine – what a treat! Just a word, while I mention Lonely Planet guides. Make sure you do not, by accident or otherwise, purchase a photocopied version. It does the same job, has the same information, but the maps have no roads only map guides and the photographs are black and white copier standard. I had purchased a Laos book, sealed, on a coach trip to Halong Bay. I was not permitted to open the packaging until I had paid and left the shop. The way to tell is to look down the side at the tabs, if they are blue, not black, it is a genuine copy.

Back to Vientaine. At its centre is Putaxi Park, which has a concrete version of something resembling the Arc De Triomphe, in Paris. This monument was erected by the Laotian people in the late sixties using cement that the Americans had sent over to build a runway for their use during the War. The Americans didn't get their runway, wondered where all the cement had gone but Vientiane had a new attraction! It was, in all fairness, situated on a very straight, two-lane carriageway, rather like the Champs Élysées or looking remarkably like a runway. Maybe the instructions were lost in translation, who knows! But I don't think so...

Laos is a country the size of the UK. I would love to wrap it up and place it on a high shelf far away from tourism. It was stunning but will quickly change as tourism continues to grow. It was made up of many ethnic minority groups – apparently sixty-eight in total although it is difficult to count them. The present government, in its wisdom, has tidied in to three groups and named them. The people were sorted into groups chosen simply by how high above sea level they resided. These minority groups have lived alongside each other, working, marrying, trading, for centuries. Traditional skills and craftwork have been essential for living and trading. They are taught from an early age. This will change as the world and the tourists intrude.

I found it to be a fascinating little pocket of a country bordered by some big neighbours, Thailand, China, Vietnam and also Cambodia and Myanmar. In the past it has been colonised by the French and financially supported by the Americans. It took time for me to discover its identity but when I did I was not disappointed. With Laos you have to look very carefully to discover its beauty, it's a slow burn.

The people are so different here to their more powerful neighbours, they are more chilled and laid back. Even driving on the roads seemed quieter without the incessant blowing of horns to let other drivers know you are overtaking them. The women work hard and certainly long hours. It was interesting, the difference really showed when booking a tour of the Plain of Jars in Phonsavan. From the pushy ticket sellers and shop holders of Vietnam, calling to every passer-by to a very quiet market where you felt relaxed enough to browse and a tour guide who happily let us go to find a better price. It was totally different. There was a lovely quote that I found in Lonely Planet used to describe the difference between Laos and its neighbouring nations. The writers use an analogy of rice production, it says that the French had a saying during their time in Asia that *'The Vietnamese plant the rice, the Cambodians tend the rice and the Lao listen to it grow.'* They are not lazy as such but there is a kind of 'whatever whenever' attitude here. The skills I had developed to fend off enthusiastic pushy vendors were no longer needed and I started to relax enough to be able to browse through their wares.

Travelling with these laid back people was great fun. It's funny how the smallest details made me laugh and feel content. I travel with a small pack of needlework to hand as I find it restful and calming, I can simply observe the passing landscape and think. But it added another dimension of contact I could never have imagined. Time and time again a local person would stop, give me a thumbs up at my work or sit by me and examine what I was doing. Many was the time I've had to backtrack a few stitches when they've had a go at it! I enjoyed conversations in two languages, no comprehension, but a real communication took place. I felt humbled.

But by far the funniest interaction was when I offered a biscuit, crisp or fruit. Whether adult or child, the whole packet would vanish: one time an empty packet was passed back. A beautiful hill tribe lady who joined me on one occasion pointed to my bottle of water, I offered her a drink of it but she headed off with the bottle! It struck me that for me it was easy, I go and get another one, for her it's not that straightforward. Also, I've noticed a few older people collecting plastic bottle so it may be that there was some form of payment for their collection, like we did as kids with the Whites lemonade bottles! On one occasion I was having a friendly exchange with a small girl, beautiful face, features and eyes but when she smiled I could see her teeth were rotten and misplaced. That wouldn't happen to our children. We are so lucky in the west.

I shared a pineapple with two teenagers who promptly threw the empty package over their shoulders into the Mekong River. The Mekong, such a mighty fine river! This was not the first time I had witnessed such mindless littering. It had been the same in Cambodia as well.

To imagine this as a communist country was very difficult, it was a beautiful rural community. It makes the bombing by the Americans in the 1960s a bigger travesty. War is always a tragedy, but Laos was the most bombed country in the world per capita. Between 1964 – 1973 the USA carried out 580,944 sorties and dropped 2,093,100 tons of bombs on Laos, especially around the Plain of Jars. The biggest and most extending problem was the use of cluster munitions, of which 270 million were dropped and something like thirty per cent failed to explode upon impact. Since 1974 20,000 people have been killed or injured – about 300 a year are still affected as to this day there are still thousands of unexposed devices killing innocent people and children long after the war is over. I visited an exhibition of work being done to clear fields and make the land safe again but this is slow progress.

A place I did love was Luang Prabang. A chilled Lao-French riverside town, so beautiful, with so many small, personal hotels, decked out in shiny wood and open fronts. Again a Lonely Planet guide had a suggested a city walk, allowing me to find my way around very easily and take in some highlights. It has a fabulous, chilled night market that was a pleasure to peruse, a real treat. I took a three-day trip through the mountains to Phonsavan to see the Plain of Jars.

Now there's a phenomenon, 3000 stone jars, scattered on high ground, no markings, no obvious deliberate layout, no explanation as to what they were, who had made them and why.

Legend would suggest many explanations from whisky goblets for the giants that roamed the land in some past time, to burial chambers before cremation. Personally, I think they were more likely to have been some sort of storage jars for traders who traversed the salt or silk trade routes of old times.

It just struck me as typical for Laos that no one had any idea and with this they were content. Our guide tried to link the jars to our own Stonehenge until I pointed out that the size, shape and precise position of the stones found in the UK was so far removed for this to be an acceptable link.

As a solo traveller it was possible to look for other single travellers and form a group. The price for a tour, with a guide to see all three tourist sites, reduced from 250,000 kip for a solo tour to 100,000 kip when there were seven of us. It was easy to spot individual or couples, they were the ones, like myself, pouring over a Lonely Planet guide, looking this way and that! A visit to Phonsavan included a visit to the MGA centre for updates on the bomb clearance and interesting film presentations. The tour provided me with a further interesting insight into the people of Laos. Ever since the war had ended scrap metal had been collected by defusing live bombs. This had been recycled into boats, spoons (loads of them), bangles, keyrings. The light metal from the bombs made an excellent recyclable, money-making product. It was just a shame that even though the people had learnt to disarm the weapons for resale there were still fatal accidents. But needs must.

An interesting discussion with our extremely laid back hostel owner suggested many theories of double dealing and underhand drug trading involving the CIA during the war. It was interesting to note that there was a strange tale to tell here. Added to this there was a 'secret village' close by which had been the American base during the war. No one was allowed to visit it without police escort, apparently an agreement for secrecy between the Laos and Amercian governments; I wonder why. There was also talk of a village of maimed victims who never left the village to enter normal society. I definitely got the feeling of something unsaid here, and most probably better that way. Despite this intrigue Phonsavan and the Plain of Jars was beautiful and well worth the hair-raising minivan ride over the mountain passes.

Travelling through Laos was just as easy as it had been in both Cambodia and Vietnam, easy to book minivans or sleeper buses. Sleeper buses do their job, getting passengers from place to place while you sleep. I consoled myself by thinking that I would enjoy some of the landscape whilst travelling through Laos by looking out of the window, but the windows of the sleeper buses are too narrow or closed off.

On the journey from Vientiane to Luang Prabang I was put off these buses totally. This bus was decked out like a series of Barbie bedrooms, pink, padded and sectioned. Each section had a small double bed. Travelling alone was a temporary problem – I had to share a bed with an unknown person. I grabbed a space, spread myself and my belongs out and stared out of the window thus avoiding eye contact with people getting on the bus. To my relief we set off and I still had my own space, until we reached Vang Vieng when the bus stopped to pick up a load of Chinese. I pretended to be asleep but eventually my little space had to be shared with a Chinese man. He was very nice and we politely accommodated each other by matching sleeping positions and turning over at the same time.

On we went into the night until the bus broke down at one a.m. In total darkness we were gestured to leave the bus and walk to the next village where a whole busload of tourists spent the night on a village doorstep, much to the inhabitants' amusement the next morning. There was one toilet, not a public toilet, which was shared by all the passengers. It was in a back yard, no light, loads of cobwebs and broken boards. To add to the drama a family of pigs and piglets joined us foraging for food and snorting.

The bus didn't get fixed and at eleven a.m. the following morning I, and some other passengers, flagged down a minivan to get to our destination. It cost a further 70,000 Kip (less than £10) and no hope of a refund or compensation. It was interesting, at times like this when things go wrong I missed our British system of information and being looked after or mollycoddled.

I decided to make the best of it and enjoy the view from the minivan, the countryside was fabulous, so green and beautiful. I fought hard to stay awake in a small seat with no headrest, only an unimpressed Dutch woman traveller on to whose shoulder I kept falling. I had only slept briefly during the night on a mat, spread out on a doorstep. But things like this happen, buses are late or full or break down.

I felt it was a measure of how relaxed I had become, not fussing about the inconvenience and rough experience but rather simply riding it out. I certainly wasn't going to waste my time getting frustrated trying to get my 70,000 kip back only to be met with 'not understanding the language' or total denial. This is not a country with high customer service standards that we tend to expect to be the norm from our side of the world. I decided at that point that I would not travel on night buses any longer but would take local buses or minivans and sit back to enjoy the view. I find to be able to look out of the window as you travel through a country provides an excellent time to think and simply observe.

It was straight after this experience with the bus that I had probably what every female solo traveller, any age, dreads, the unwanted, persistent attention of a solo male traveller. He was on the bus that rescued us, he gave me food (I was starving!) and made a fuss of me, which was lovely after the previous evening. I shared his offering with another Laos lady who had suffered the same fate as me and we soon had offerings from everyone on the bus. They were so welcome. He invited me out to dinner that evening. I agreed to go, treating the invite with the same approach as I would any fellow traveller, simply sharing a meal and conversation. We shared a bottle of wine and shared the bill.

I was straight with him, telling him I was spoken for and very happy, making it very obvious from the outset that this was going no further than a pleasant conversation and a meal. However, he tried insisting that I join him on his travels, or at least go with him to the night market or ATM. After much persistence he eventually accepted defeat, I'd like to say with some grace. Thankfully, he had booked a tour to the Plain of Jars the next morning and said he would have dinner again with me in three days' time. Phew, I thought, that's the end of that, until he knocked on my room door three days later. The first couple of times I ignored him. The next morning he knocked again, asking me to come to breakfast.

He was not staying in my hotel and I was frankly alarmed at the security of my hotel to allow this gentleman access to my door on two occasions. Later that day, in the market, I bumped into a guy I had travelled with briefly in Vietnam. I hugged him in relief and went for a glass of wine. It was good to be treated as a person and have a comfortable conversation. Funny how different people can be. I was at the time a bit disturbed by the unwanted attention but felt happy with the way I had dealt with it. If there were any hard feelings I did not feel I was to blame.

I had my first experience of spending the day with elephants in Laos. It was expensive but worth every penny, or rather cent, to spend the day with these beautiful creatures. I managed a bare back, clumsy, scary ride towards the end of the day but thoroughly enjoyed my day with them. This was a highlight for me. The problem with doing anything with elephants in this part of the world is that so many of these beautiful creatures are beaten to perform or comply. I asked about the living standards and found that each elephant had their own mahout or trainer and that was who looked after them. They were taken into the jungle to sleep at night although a long chain was attached to each of them to prevent them from roaming or falling in to the hands of poachers. I hope I made a wise choice. The elephants were all relaxed and there was no evidence of sticks or other ways to train the animals.

There's lots of building going on in Laos, especially elephant parks and mountain slides. But what will become of the traditional way of the life? The traditional craft skills passed down from generation to generation? The ethnic minority groups? There was a good deal of work, small groups, volunteer and charity funding working to teach traditional skills to women and address this issue by raising awareness of the importance of the handed down craft skills. This will be lost.

I left Laos a happier traveller than the one who had arrived. I had seen its soft underbelly, appreciated its charms but also detected a need to leave well alone. There's more to this country than meets the eye. I said farewell to the lovely Luang Prabang on a slow boat headed for Thailand as an access point for Myanmar. I wondered with some regret if I had cut Laos short. I had intended to travel down south to the hammock paradise of the 4000 Islands at Don Det. But with Thailand reachable by river two days away I decided to change my route.

That is another bonus of travelling alone, you can please yourself and go where you want to, when you want to. I intend to return to Laos at some point to see the southern bit I missed, probably from a trip to Cambodia. But at that moment my main interest was in a slightly less travelled Myanmar. There are no land borders between Laos and its neighbouring Myanmar. So off up the river I went, spending two complete days on a river that has fascinated me for a long time, the Mekong. There was an overnight stopover in the old and quite primitive village of Pakbeng. I stayed slightly outside the main village, in a hostel up the hill and had a rice dish in a converted garage. It made the evening special to grab a beer and watch the sun set over the river. There was a steep slope to get up to get up to the village. This was difficult after negotiating a narrow plank to disembark from the boat to the bank. There were pigs squealing as they were being weighed before being sold. It was like being in a different world.

The boat was a long slow boat used mainly by locals to travel up the river to Pakbeng, which provided the overnight stop over point, or on to the border. The river was fast flowing at some points and had low points where rocks were visible above the water. I loved watching the life along the riverbanks, families playing, children waving at the boat, fishing in the water or doing laundry. It was a great way to spend two days travelling and watching the local people go about their daily lives.

I had fun at the border. The boat trip ended on the Laos side of the Mekong and to get to Thailand I had to find a tuk tuk to take me across the Friendship Bridge to the Thai border. I didn't have any Thai baht and I had just given all of my Laos currency to a lady who had been on the boat with me. I did have some dollars though and after some haggling I got a driver to take me across. I had to walk across the border in the rain. It was dark and I was cold. I was only wearing flip flops and my feet were wet. It was the evening of my birthday and I felt quite alone. Onwards

North Thailand

Chiang Khong – Chiang Rai – Chiang Mai – Phitsanalouk – Kohn Kaen – Nong Wa

Thailand is the friendly face of South-East Asia. It was easy to travel around, most people speak English, and tourism well organised. Westerners are welcome and accepted. There are many trips available to explore the highlights from the main tourist cities. It was a doddle as far as solo travel was concerned. I arrived at the Thai border after a leisurely cruise down the Mekong. It was my birthday. I knew it was going to be a strange day, it being my birthday and being used to the people around me knowing and acknowledging that fact. I know it was a small matter in the grand scheme of things, but nevertheless.

I had plenty of messages via email, WhatsApp, messenger and Facebook but no one had wished me a happy birthday verbally, so I could hear it. I really missed that. But what was I to do? Announce the occasion to my fellow travellers or wear a badge? At the end of the journey from Laos I was having a lovely conversation, by gesture, with an old lady; we shared no common language. She was beautiful but extremely poor. She was eating sticky rice by the handful from a hessian sack that was stowed under the seats. She had a beautiful face and smile but rotten teeth. She was examining my crochet work.

I decided to tell her that it was my birthday, so I used Google translate to convey the message about it being my birthday. She looked at my phone, gestured, laughed and then it struck me that she could not read, even in her own language. I had failed in my one attempt to get some attention and I felt ashamed of myself. It struck me in my guilt that she would probably never have enough money in her lifetime to take a plane ride out of her country to visit another and here was I travelling around with complete freedom and financial resources. I gave her some money.

I am pleased to say that going through customs over the Thai border the customs officer wished me 'Happy birthday' as he stamped my passport, I could have kissed him! The other funny thing that happened at the border going out of Laos was the officer asking me to pay for overtime. I was indignant and replied that I had not overstayed my visa, in fact I was leaving Laos before the end of the current visa. We had the same conversation three times before I realised he wanted me to pay him an extra charge of 40 baht (70p) because he was on overtime as it was Sunday evening. Apparently, this was normal practice.

One of the interesting challenges on a trip like this was keeping up with the switching of currencies and their respective values against the pound. How much was I spending? I had learnt my lesson from going to the ATM in Vietnam without knowing how much to withdraw and what was the fair price for a taxi. In Thailand, the lesson was different. The Thai currency, the Baht, does not have the endless, confusing noughts that the previous neighbouring countries had. I found myself nearly handing over a fortune in my ignorance in a shoe shop. The ladies who served me were excellent and quickly pointed out my mistake. I needed to think in hundreds now and not thousands. I will remain ever thankful for their honesty but this cannot lessen the feeling of foolishness for having made such a mistake. I downloaded a Google app to work out the value of what I was spending until I was able to do the calculation myself.

I followed the main tourist route through Thailand, visiting Chiang Rai and Chiang Mai, taking organised tours to see the highlights. This was easy but worked out more expensive and I really missed the added value of a good guide! Some of the guides were very friendly but did not provide a great deal of information about the places we were visiting.

An example of this was the visit to the White Temple, which was a white folly needing, to my mind, some explanation as to what the references are and what the artist was hoping to achieve. There were only two of us on the tour so I felt our guide had no excuse not to provide interesting commentary. If you ever visit the White Temple you will probably understand where I am coming from. I bought a book and read it in the back of the mini bus and then clearly understood the intention of the artist and was able to appreciate his work. I found that the problem with organised tours was that you can get presented with a somewhat false view of the country.

I went to see a hill tribe village. It was fascinating to see the Karen women, the long neck women, and see for myself the rings around their necks. Interestingly, their necks are no longer than normal but the rings, due to their weight, sink in to the collar and shoulder bones, rendering the neck muscles useless should the rings ever be taken off, which they are not. But I got the impression this was a set up for the tourists, like walking through a human zoo. I felt uncomfortable and bought endless tack from each trader to assuage my feelings of guilt and discomfort, which may have been their intention anyway! But like most things in Thailand it didn't cost a fortune…

Thai food was amazing; fresh, zesty, hot and simple. I found that eating with local people offered the most variety and certainly the cheapest options. I began to get used to, even look forward to, spicy noodles or rice porridge with pork for breakfast and there was no need for lunch. However, it never ceased to amaze me how much these Thai people tuck away each day and still remain bird-like and slim. I found a place serving Eggs Benedict for breakfast but soon realised I was spending a day's food budget on one meal so headed back to the plastic chairs and tables of the street vendors. Frequently, and worryingly, eating utensils get washed together in one large bowl of doubtful looking water. Fortunately I did not to suffer from any bouts of food poisoning or stomach upsets so I guess everything was okay.

I travelled by local bus through Thailand. This was amazingly cheap – about £2 to £3 for a six-hour trip through beautiful scenery, and free water, biscuits and lunch. I will admit there were a variety of buses offering different levels of comfort, I could have sworn one of them had wooden wheels! The people were friendly and helpful, everyone wanting to show me the right bus, help me to my seat (Please, do I look that much in need!), carry my bag and get me to the right ticket counter. There seemed to be no shortage of these 'helpers' around. It can be confusing using the local bus route though as many cities and towns have numerous bus stations and you need to get to the right one. I usually managed to find a window seat and have two seats to myself, I spent many a happy trip listening to Roger Waters or The Script on my headphones whilst looking at the passing scenery through the window. Such a cheap and pleasurable way to travel.

In each country I have stayed in cheap hostels or hotels. Each costing between £7 to £20 a night, often including breakfast. But in each country I allowed myself a treat, a night in a nice hotel, preferably with a pool to relax beside. It became obvious to me that I needed to stop on occasions and catch my breath as it was a temptation to be constantly travelling, on the go. It was necessary to make myself stop and take stock. In Thailand I booked a room with a bath, for two nights. I did nothing for two days but sat by the pool, ate and read in the bath. A real treat. Restored, I moved on from this hotel to a room in Kohn Kaen where I paid 440 baht (£8.03) for two nights. The difference between the two hotels made me laugh out loud yet there was a part of me that wanted to run back to luxury but I knew I had to make sacrifices to afford the occasional luxury. This was only one of the two hotels when I made use of my own bedding I had brought with me from home and settled down for night's kip. My trusty Lonely Planet guide had described it as being one of the oldest hotels in town, clinging to it former glory but clean. Hmmm... the glory was certainly former!

I ended this leg of my Thailand trip staying with friends in Nong Wa, about five hours by road from Bangkok. It was lovely just to relax. The usual concerns of where and how to get next or where to stay or eat were temporarily put aside. I was made extremely welcome and spent ten days with them. I was the only farang lady in the village!

It was lovely being part of a quiet farming village and I got quite settled into the group activities. I took part in local craft activities and even ended up accepting a position in a local school to teach English later on in the year. This was perfect, I got to stay with friends, work and gain new experiences.

However, I noticed a settling down, a taming, a losing of the desire to travel, discover, move on, which was the whole point of this year. I had a plan, a route through SE Asia to complete. The teaching experience in November was perfect timing as I could complete my intended travel plans. I organised a visa for Myanmar, booked a plane ticket and headed back out to the trail, so to speak!

I felt slightly despondent travelling to the airport, worried again about travelling on alone. This was something I hadn't experienced for a while, I had rarely felt concerned or lonely travelling right through Cambodia, Vietnam and Laos. This feeling surprised me but I pushed on and boarded the flight out of the perceived safety of Thailand to the less travelled Myanmar.

The flight was extremely bumpy with passengers being thrown up several feet from their seats during turbulence. Monks were silently praying in the seats across from me, I did not find that in the least reassured by them and prepared myself for the worst. If it all came to end now everything was organised at home and my travel insurance would cover the rest. But we made it and I jumped in to a taxi heading for the outskirts of a very busy, damp Yangon and suddenly felt alive again. All about Myanmar next. Onwards.

Myanmar

Myanmar was an unusual experience. I loved it and hated it in equal measure. I was expecting a really different experience of this SE Asian country. It seemed that everyone who had been, or was thinking of going, loved it. It was a place that has been concealed and protected by its ruling government from the eyes of the outside world. Tourism has not been encouraged and the media kept under strict control. Even a major disaster like the aftermath of a cyclone hitting the country was minimised to prevent the eyes of the world being on Myanmar. This country has been under tight media censorship since 1962. Every effort was made by the military to close Burma, as it was then known, off from the outside in and from the inside out.

I remember when thinking about this trip wondering when Burma had been renamed Myanmar. I had always known it as Burma but apparently in 2011, along with changing other British names for places such as Rangoon to Yangon. The military changed it without consent or consultation with its people. Yet, when talking to individual locals working in the hotels or tours, they referred to themselves as Burmese.

I found the history of this land fascinating, probably more so due to the fact that it had been part of the British Empire at one point. Colonial good and bad points are worth discussing but beyond my intention here. It was worth looking up the history to gain a further understanding of Myanmar today, especially concerning its borders and problematic minority groups. It was a fascinating, colourful country, beautiful and in some ways time-locked and not without its problems.

I learnt a few days later that a cyclone had been in the area causing damage in India and inches of rain to Myanmar. After we landed, shaken but somewhat glad to be in one piece I grabbed a taxi and headed to a hotel I had booked online.

I can remember looking out of the taxi window and being enthralled by my surroundings. It was damp, sodden, dark green, snarled up with traffic and every man without exception was wearing a longyi, which is a wrap around, full-length skirt. It looked so different from anywhere I had so far experienced. I looked forward to exploring and finding out more about this unusual place.

The first evening I ate locally, sitting on a plastic chair at a plastic table, eating dried rice and dried something else, sipping a beer and being openly stared at by everyone around me. I did not feel uncomfortable but rather enjoyed my new surroundings. In contrast to my earlier lack-lustre feelings leaving Thailand I felt really alive again and ready to explore, I loved being somewhere new and strange.

There was a power cut, street vendors used candles to light their stalls, everything else was in pitch darkness. I used a torch to check my footing on the way back to my hotel. Apparently power cuts were not unusual in this country.

The following day I got in a taxi and literally sailed through the flooded streets to down town Yangon. The taxi driver had no English and I just pointed to a place listed in the guide book with the most guest houses in the area. He dropped me and my rucksack off at The Strand! This hotel was the most expensive hotel in Myanmar, cheaper than our London high-end hotels, but more expensive than what I had been paying. I walked into the lobby, it was beautiful, wooden parquet floors, beautiful red quality carpeting, palms, impeccably dressed and mannered staff, it felt like I stepped into 1940s colonial Britain, had Poirot followed me in he would not have looked out of place. The lift had teak flooring, each staircase was wide and grand and there was a butler to each floor and three pin plugs!

I decided that this hotel was going to be my treat for Myanmar but for one night only. I paid a basic package and was immediately upgraded with breakfast included. I had a suite of rooms I could have happily moved into for the rest of my life. The bathroom was old-fashioned white quality tiles, a separate bath and shower, luxury bath sheets unlike the smelly stiff ones I had experienced previously in other hotels and guest houses. It was pure and utter luxury. I realised I would have an issue spending so much on one night on myself. However, I had a simple agreement with myself that I would have one luxury stay in each country I visited. It had been good enough for Rudyard Kipling and Somerset Maugham, I was sure it would be good enough for me.

Everyday expenses were so cheap out here and I was spending less than I was earning in the UK, so an occasional luxury was fine; it's all part of deciding on a budget, what my limit was, what my requirements were and going with it.

I explored the streets of the local area. They were hazardous, soaked, and with gaping holes from open sewage work. These had been dug up and left exposed, with no warning signs or fall prevention signage. The old, once beautiful colonial buildings were blackened with moss and mildew. Such a sorry state.

One of the streets was lined with second hand books stalls, with great stacks of books; where did they all come from? I bought a book called *Finding George Orwell in Burma* by Emma Larkin. It provided a dark and interesting insight into the life of this colonial policeman and his works, which had been heavily influenced by his time in Burma.

The rain hammered down at one point and I sheltered with a Burmese man under some tarpaulin. He politely offered to escort me to my hotel under his umbrella but I was very conscious that I was staying in a place that was probably equivalent to more than a month's wages to these poor people. With regret, I politely declined his generous offer.

The next day I walked to the railway station, another past glory colonial building, and booked my ticket up through the heart of the country and across to Bagan, stopping at Taungoo and Thazi on the way. The ticket was handwritten in ink on paper that looked like old certificate paper. But the best experience was yet to come... I chose train travel as a way of getting to see the real Myanmar, off the beaten track, and that's exactly what happened!

That afternoon, after sorting out my train ticket, I visited the wonderful Shwedagon Paya and was not disappointed with its majesty and beauty. It was wonderfully constructed and decorated in gold with precious stones adorning the walls. The floor was spotlessly clean and tiled. I did feel, not for the first time, that there was a sharp contrast between the condition of ordinary housing and the sacred quality extended to these religious sites. No betel spitting or littering in these sacred places. They are beautifully kept with many families spending whole day picnicking on the floors to escape the heat in the cool temple courts.

The next morning the train trundled, literally trundled, slowly out of Yangon at six am. I had left the paradise pocket in The Strand to stay nearer the train station in a room with no window. This was in a hotel, which was a fraction of the price but a fraction of the experience. The city passed by my open window, messy, dirty, overcrowded, poor, basically a depressing sight. Parts of it were flooded, most parts were just covered in litter. Bleak. The excess rainfall had soaked some areas, others were submerged in a few feet of water. The train rocked, jumped, rocked again, it was like being in a horse and cart. But this was the experience I wanted. The trains themselves are old, somewhat uncomfortable but the open windows allow passengers to hang out of them, which I loved, providing a cool breeze and a closer look at my surroundings. From what I could see life was abundant around the track and the stations. The toilet was a hole in the floor through which you could see the passing track. It took several attempts for me to perfect my balance in order to use this facility and also avoid being knocked senseless by having my head hit on the side of the cubicle by the violent rocking from side to side of the train movement. To add terror to the experience was the threat of being tossed from the train through the open doors on the opposite side of the entrance to the carriage. All part of the fun!

Life along the train tracks provided endless, interesting sights from washing laid on the grass land beside the track to goats being herded and the cheeky smiles from waving children. I was the only foreigner travelling on the train, certainly the only white skinned, blonde, lone female and it seemed that everyone greeted me, smiled, adjusted my window during downpours of rain and informed me when I was due to get off. This was useful, if not a little unnerving, as everyone seemed to know where I was going.

My first stop was Taungoo. A lady helped me alight and find a trishaw driver to take me to my guesthouse. Another bumpy, jerky ride in a too small and hard seat. The whole experience of Taungoo was uncomfortable and for the first time I felt vulnerable. This may have been an overreaction on my part after reading of Orwell's time in Burma as a policeman. But I felt like everyone was watching me, knew where I was going and where I was staying.

The hotel was small, out of town and the room was damp, including the bed and bed linen. I used bedding from home for the second time this trip and pushed my locking doorstop under the door before going to sleep. I went out to eat but after being completely ignored for at least fifteen minutes, and being stared at, I left the restaurant. I crossed the road to a shack selling food. I sat down to eat dried chicken and rice, at least I think that was what it was.

Again I was the centre of attention and a betel chewing man joined me at my table. My table was a low plastic stool and equally low plastic table. God knows what I was eating but it came with a variety of pickles and, what only can be described as 'bits'. My betel chewing companion had red lips and black, decaying teeth, which were on full view when he smiled. He was, however, very pleasant to me. He spat out red juice on the floor beside us, each spit was preceded by a loud, guttural noise in his throat, which was enough to make me excuse myself to make a quick exit back to my damp, unwelcoming room for an early night.

I purchased two beers, claiming one was for my friend who was not feeling well and waiting in the hotel room. But in reality what was the point of such a blatant fib when everyone for certain seemed to have noticed me and realised I was alone. I left, checking behind me at intervals to make sure nobody was following me and returned to my sad hotel room for an early night, thanking God for my Kindle!

I continued on the train the next morning. Life on the station was colourful and busy. The platforms were filled with women and children, many of whom must spend their lives on stations or on trains selling their wares. Large platters of homemade snacks are piled high and carried on their heads. This makes easy service to train windows. Full credit to these hard working people for making the most of every opportunity to sell anything! I was greatly cheered by a group of chattering women sharing lunch with me on the platform whilst waiting for my train.

At beginning of the day you can depend on most trains being on time but delays build up during the day, I was waiting in the middle of the day so the hour wait for the scheduled train was nothing in this part of the world. The women happily passed around food and their babies for me to hold, they pinched my skin and took photos of me. The attention was gentle and welcome, their faces smeared with white powder to make them appear white and protect their skin from the sun. Back on the train which trundled, literally trundled, along to Thazi.

This time I was taken to my hotel through the dark, muddy streets by horse and cart. This whole experience of being off the beaten track felt as if I had stepped off the world into another time. It was an incredible experience, both frightening and exciting, I was having the experience I had hoped for. This time I stayed in a very basic hostel, clean, welcoming but yes, very basic! No window in the room, towel strung on a piece of string, light switch mounted picture-rail height, choice of shower temperature cold or cold, coupled with drying off using a towel that had the feel and appearance of a dry chamois leather.

There were only two guesthouses to choose from, the one I stayed in or the government guesthouse next door. Despite basic conditions I think I made the right choice. The owners were lovely. Their grandparents had set up the guesthouse after WWII, coming from India. They settled in Thazi due solely to the fact that there was a train station there! I had a long chat with the owner. She was extremely open about the conditions of living here in Myanmar. She spoke of the unfairness that operated between those that work for the government and those that don't. It would seem that things haven't changed that much, if at all.

I noticed that we had sat away from other listening ears, but maybe I'd been reading too much about the atmosphere that existed not so long ago of listeners, informers and political prisoners.

The people were friendly. They are more reserved than others in this part of the world but time and time again I would smile or wave first to be rewarded with warmth in return. They have been through tough times, times when it was impossible to trust authority or each other. They are diligent in their approach to work, having excellent craft skills in woodcarving, stone carving and gems.

I left Thazi the next morning happier and feeling safer. The temporary feeling of contentment was quickly shattered when the police were waiting at the station to check my ticket and escort me to my seat, then rechecking to make sure I was still sitting there a while later. As a foreigner it was necessary to travel on upper class from Yangon but sat on ordinary class to Bagan. I had an official escort all the way to the end of the line, sitting two seats in front of me, to make sure I got to where my ticket stated. The train trundled on, yes again trundled, and I tried to be realistic and settle to enjoy the passing countryside, trying not to react and become uncomfortable with the unwarranted, also unwelcome surveillance. The view passing my window was beautiful, changing all the time from flooded paddy fields to dry pineapple fields and palm trees.

On arriving at Bagan station it would seem that word had gone ahead that there was a tourist on the train. I stood up from my seat to collect my bag and turned around to find that a taxi driver had jumped in through the open train window and was stood directly behind me, with another taxi driver running up the aisle of the train to me to get my fare! I had to laugh but they do all have to fight for all the income and this actually broke the spell of feeling unwelcome, I was grateful to them in that moment for their unexpected attention.

After all the exposure and unwanted attention journeying by train I broke my intention of having just one treat in each country. For the second time in Myanmar I went off budget and booked a spa resort. In all fairness I had a reasonably good off-peak price, enjoyed the pool, nice wine in nice glasses and a couple of hours with a monk to restore my equilibrium. On reflection, where I stayed had a direct impact on how safe I felt and my entire experience of each place. The lower end guesthouse is a bit potluck but you do get a real sense of where you are and the people who live there. Higher end, more expensive places can be a wonderful break but in reality you could be anywhere in the world. Interestingly, I felt more isolated and lonely in more expensive places as I tended to encounter more couples, groups and families, seeing less solo travellers. For me, I enjoyed the mix of good and bad, cheap and more expensive.

During my time at the resort I was joined for dinner by a lovely forty-four year old Malaysian university teacher, educated in India but living in Canada. He did not chew or spit betel, didn't throw litter and we enjoyed a long dinner together with good conversation. He moved on the next day but I bumped into him again a week later at Mandalay airport, boarding a plane to Bangkok.

Bagan was amazing. Timeless, fascinating, a delight for tourist and photographer alike, so much to see. It was amazing to explore by hiring a bicycle and pottering between the temples alone. I did go on an organised tour although I would have done just as well myself and saved a good deal of money. Bagan was geared up for the tourist and was a total contrast to my recent days traveling on a train through central Myanmar. It was very tame by comparison. I enjoyed the pool and the view of the Irrawaddy flowing, or rather over-flowing past the end of the garden. I booked a bus to make my way to Mandalay. The service, as I had found all over SE Asia, was cheap and excellent.

Mandalay, just the mention of such a place brings to mind, well brings to mind what exactly? The road to Mandalay – inspiring, exotic but in reality dusty, bumpy, disappearing in places and far from the Mandalay made famous by Kipling in his poem of the same name. Mandalay itself was a shock. Dirty, chaotic, busy, wet. I had met a New Zealand guy in Chiang Rai, Thailand who had recommended a hotel just outside the city and far enough removed from the city itself to be comfortable. He was right and I benefitted from my stay there. I enjoyed a city tour with a guide and did the usual touristy things. The sacred sites were amazing, rich in culture and gold! Climbing up and down Mandalay Hill was a real delight and worth the forty-five minute walk.

I had planned to move on by local bus to Inle Lake in order to complete my visit to Myanmar but on seeing the city's roads turned fast to flowing rivers I cancelled the bus and jumped on a plane headed for the relative familiarity and comfort that is Bangkok. I was glad to escape Myanmar, not certain if I would ever return but glad I had been. Marmite, that's how I remember Myanmar, you either love it or hate it.

I really struggled writing up this chapter and had to leave what I had written for a week before I looked at it again. I was upset and confused that Myanmar had disturbed me so much, I had loved bits of it but it was certainly not the experience I had expected to have. It had the best hotels I have stayed in so far and the worst guesthouses. The attention from the authorities was not one I welcomed or was used to but there was another fact that came in to play.

As a solo traveller I had found that all my senses were working overtime. On the very last day in the country, half an hour before I was due to move from Mandalay to enjoy Inle Lake I felt a clear message/feeling/instruction to leave and leave now. I went with this gut feeling and headed immediately to Mandalay airport, not even having time enough to book a seat on a plane. I took a taxi through streets knee high in water. People were pushing motorbikes through water flowing halfway above their wheels, engines broken down from being flooded. Children were jumping about in the water as if they were enjoying themselves at the local pool! It was an incredible sight. Unfortunately for the people of Myanmar severe flooding, of an epidemic scale, was to follow.

On arriving at the airport sales counter I bumped in to a young American who had had her purse stolen in Bagan. She was distressed, standing at the counter, counting and recounting her money, desperately trying to make 34000 Kyat into 150000 Kyat needed for a flight to Thailand. I felt for her in her plight, and anxious state. I paid for her ticket as well as mine. There have been many occasions on my journey when my immediate needs had been met by strangers and I believe firmly that this was the time I was meant to meet her immediate needs by buying her a plane ticket out.

I have talked to others who have travelled alone and this has been their experience too. I refer to them as 'travel angels' because maybe that's exactly what they are, who knows? Regardless of whether I see my money again or not was secondary to the point as I felt I had received help so often that this was my turn to give back.

I was so disturbed by the urgent need to leave Mandalay that I discussed this with a number of close friends who helped me put things back in to perspective once again. I concluded that it was all part of being on my own, I got a full sense of everything, good or bad. It was essential that I had support from friends who can quickly comprehend what has happened and are able to support appropriately. I am grateful to my support group. It was at that time when things went wrong that I was able to learn what I was capable of and these experiences will last a lifetime.

In addition to the traumatic departure from Myanmar, I had been upset by the poverty and filth I had seen, coupled with a total disregard of people to do anything for themselves by way of disposing of litter in bins and not spitting all over pavements in public areas. Not only does either of these two bad habits add to the poor conditions but what of public health? The other aspect that had disturbed me greatly was their apparent lack of care for animals. Dogs, mangy, pathetic, skinny dogs roamed the streets and pavements. The cattle and goats were just skin and bone. An initiative to feed or at least control the number of these poor, helpless creatures was surely possible, wasn't it?

Myanmar was the last pearl of Asia to open its borders to the outside world. This showed. Maybe with a change of government and attitude of its people to observe simple acts of cleanliness will make a huge difference. Having said that it was possible to avoid its less desirable underbelly by simply flying internally to the highlights. Maybe there is some hope if Aung San Suu Kyi is allowed political power after a long history of banishment and house arrest.

For now progress can be encouraged and financed by tourism. Certainly keeping the country open to tourists will increase the pressure to observe a basic level of human rights and provide less opportunity for injustices to be done. It would be a positive move to see a fair election process take place. Anything could happen. I did see enough to arouse an interest for me to return, I think may be in ten years' time… who knows!

A child in a poor village in Siem Reap, Cambodia. The tourist hotels are less than a mile away.

Monkeys playing in Northern Thailand

Monks in Myanmar

A day with an Elephant in Laos

A temple in Luang Prabang

Floating markets on the Mekong Delta

Train travel through Myanmar

Chocolate, the elephant!

Ancient stone carving in Cambodia

Christmas in a Thai Village

Plain of Jars, Laos

Planting rice by hand

On the road to Mandalay....

Travelling in to Thailand from Laos in a slow boat on the Mekong

Beautiful Bagan, Myanmar

Temples as far as you can see….Bagan, Myanmar

A typical stone carving from SE Asia

A golden representation of Buddha teaching in Cambodia

The beautiful Bagan skyline

Stone temple with golden roof, Bagan

The view from Bokor mountain, Cambodia

Mandalay district surrounded by floading

Myanmar

A happy pupil in Korbua School, Thailand

Ta Prohm, a temple in Angkor, Cambodia

A folly in Vientiane

Travelling through Loas

Thailand Part 2 – Heading South

Bangkok – Hua Hin – Koh Samai – Phuket –Krabi – Railay – Hat Yai

Looking out of the plane window on the approach to Bangkok felt like a sort of homecoming. After the experience and exit from Myanmar I found the sight of Thailand very welcome. In fact, I felt so 'at home' that I jumped onto a local bus and headed for the BTS sky train, saving taxi or tuk tuk fares, to get to my hotel. I successfully arrived in Nana station close to my hotel for the weekend, feeling very proud of myself, only to be scuppered by confusing the exits from the station and getting lost in the street where the hotel was. As the saying goes, pride comes before a fall! I had only been there three times and each time I made the same mistake. I memorised the exit for future reference.

The hotel I have used in Bangkok has a fabulous sky bar that I like to visit and just stare across the city, watching the sunset and the lights of the city come on. From this elevated position I could watch the sky train coming and going, as well as listen to the sounds from the bar has an outside balcony I could hear the sounds of the traffic and music from the street below. It had in the past been reasonably priced but on this occasion the price soared. I hadn't booked and was told the hotel was full. I was so disappointed as this meant no sky bar experience!

I sat down in the lobby and signed on to an internet hotel booking site, booked myself in for the weekend. I returned to the desk with my reservation. The late booking probably hiked the price up along with the hotel being packed with people from Kuwait. The weekend was spent enjoying the sky bar, reading and much needed maintenance for hair, nails, face and, yes, an essential massage.

I was ready to hit the road again. I had found it was a temptation, when travelling, to be always travelling, moving on, learning from your local environment, visiting interesting places. But I was beginning to understand that sometimes it is good just to pull in, stop, and just simply rest in luxury.

How often do we say 'It's a small world!' during this trip? I have made many friends with whom I will remain in contact and I will meet again, others who stay for a while and then drift away, but there are friends that move around too, and sometimes you have the luxury of being away from home but in the same place, at the same time. This happened in Bangkok. I met for dinner with a Thai friend who had stayed with us in Cardiff and two friends from Brighton. That's another pleasure of international travelling, impromptu dinners with friends travelling too.

The train network through southern Thailand was first class. Bangkok central station was spotless, the trains are shiny and clean. Each train had a train captain in a smart uniform unlike our guards at home. I made my way from my little place of luxury to book a ticket to Hua Hin.

My trip from the airport may have sounded confident but I somehow managed to get lost again on the BTS train to the main station, despite there being only two lines through the city. But I was determined not to give up and jump in a taxi, I eventually made it. I changed lines at the very station the bomb hit the following week.

I boarded the train south to find that I had my own berth, complete with sink! I had purchased a first class ticket that had cost around £6 for this leg of the journey. I boarded the 15.10 train which finally departed at 17.25. The journey out of Bangkok revealed crowded slums very close to the train tracks, little alleyway neighbourhoods. There was the usual endless supply of food provided by vendors coming up and down the train at intervals. It was during this holiday that I developed a liking for hot, sweet, milky coffee as opposed to my normal black coffee. Travel by train or bus within SE Asia was so easy, so convenient, usually comfortable and cheap. This journey, despite the delayed departure, was no exception.

I arrived refreshed in Hua Hin. I booked a reasonable hotel near the beach and just enjoyed being on the beach. I booked a couple of tours to investigate the local area. One trip took me to a lovely vineyard, which not only had fabulous wine but a fantastic cheese selection to go with it. Heaven! The other day trip was spent in a beautiful national park among water reeds and mangrove walks. I have encountered many people on this trip who done small things for me but which have made such a difference.

At the national park there was an ancient guide who asked if I had been in the cave. I hadn't because I was afraid, afraid of being alone in the cave. Walking through the walkways alone had frightened me enough, there was no way I was going clambering in a cave on my own! He took me into the cave, up through a steep entrance and explained what was in the cave. I was fine until he pointed out spiders and creatures that scuttled away from our torchlights. Caves are not for the faint-hearted but he had enabled me to experience the wonder of the cave. I was grateful for this small act.

It was amusing writing up these experiences that I could have been daft enough to follow a man, alone, away from the main highway into a cave. I can only say that, as on other times during this year, I was extremely sensitive as to what would be safe and what wouldn't.

It rained after the cave visit, and when it rains out there it really rains, accompanied normally by lightning and loud claps of thunder. My taxi driver did his best to fill the rest of the day by taking me to the zoo. This was not my idea of a day trip but I forced myself to watch a snake show to face a fear of snakes. The elephants were made to play football and throw darts; is there really any need? Is that really entertainment? The problem with being a sole traveller was that if there are not any organised tours to join locally it was possible to arrange solo trips but these are usually more expensive and are not guided tours.

From Hua Hin I took a bus and boat to Koh Samui, a beautiful holiday island. The trip across to the island was a treat in itself, a smooth, fast ride on a catamaran. The only problem was with a boat full of cases and rucksacks, no storage and no system for depositing or collecting it. I had to literally stand my ground in a pushing queue and fish for my belongings from a huge stack. On the tourist route I was labelled up according to my destination. These labels fall off very easily or I would end up wearing it all day even though I had reached my destination. They are irritating, especially when they count for nothing when you've lost the little piece of paper you've been given as a ticket.

I lost my boat ticket on the way to Koh Samui and even though I was all labelled up and my luggage tagged with my destination I had to buy another ticket to get on the boat. I later found my ticket in my bag! I used all my money on another ticket and did not have any money to pay for a taxi on the other side. This would not normally be a problem, just a simple trip to a cash machine would solve it, but on arriving at Koh Samui everyone was issued tickets for organised, shared taxis which are purchased during the boat ride. I was given a ticket and sticker for the taxi. After withdrawing money I attempted to pay for my taxi fare. I tried several times but no one seemed to know what I was talking about. So I accepted karma and had a free taxi ride to my hotel to make up for the 'lost' boat ticket!

Koh Samui was a beautiful island, lovely beaches, paradise. Every now again the pure joy of doing a trip such as this hits me full pelt, I am overwhelmed with wonder and gratitude. This was such a time. I relaxed completely and appreciated the small things in life, which for me was finding coffee making facilities available, but in addition to finding three sachets available instead of the standard two. I took the opportunity to re-read two books I had enjoyed a few years back, and lay on the beach completely absorbed. I even forgot to take photographs!

It was during this stay that I was eating in the restaurant alone, no other guests to share the beach or pool with. The music in the restaurant played a Bridget Jones song from the film by the same name. As 'All by Myself' belted through the music system I was very tempted to jump up and sing it the way she does in the movie! Did I or didn't I? I'll leave that to you to decide!

Thailand is known for its lively offer, offering anything for any taste, cheaply and happily. It is not known as the 'land of smiles' for nothing. Tourism is the name of the game here and it's a game played well. It's a relaxed and safe country to travel through. I took a big tourist bus to Phuket and looking at the countryside from the window I noticed not only how stunning the country was, with its endless pineapple plantations and lime rock stacks punctuating the land, but also how well and healthy it looked. The animals were all well fed and healthy compared to what I had witnessed in Myanmar. The difference was shocking. It really was a pleasant experience.

Ahhh, Phuket, the little holiday isle in the Andaman Sea, the opposite side of the land to the Koh threesome nestling in the Gulf of Thailand I had come from. Here I came across a lot of Australians and Welsh, yes, kinfolk from Swansea and Caerphilly. A group of young men from Caerphilly greeted me like an old friend, something that would never have happened back home! I loved the chilled ambience of Phuket. Yet this was Thailand remember, and you get anything you want, if you choose to look for it, in fact here there's no need to look – it will find you.

I was sat down to dinner one evening and a young Australian lad on the next table asked if he could join me. I was surprised and somewhat put off by his drunk friend. But I agreed to him joining me whilst his friend stayed put, apparently not noticing his friend had left him. After my initial wariness of my latest new friend I settled back to an enjoyable discussion about travel and being in Phuket. I think he was overwhelmed by the continual groping he had experienced from women in the pubs and clubs, just wanting a friendly chat to a safe female. His friend did join us eventually; very handsome he was too. He was as polite and interesting as his mate. The conversation lapsed at this point and his friend went off to smoke.

It was always a pleasure being invited to or being joined by an interesting person on this solo journey but this occasion will always go down in my memory as being one of the most pleasurable, as when my dinner companion got up to leave me to join his friend, he said his farewell and then came to my side of the table and kissed me on the cheek. What a gift! So unexpected and so very welcome.

The room I stayed in during my visit to Phuket was memorable, with each room decked out to match the year being used as a room number. Needless to say I opted for 1961, my year. What really raised an eyebrow was the spelling mistake on the minibar list, 'cock' rather than coke was on offer for 50 baht, diet ones at that! Well as I said, this was Phuket... It was during this stay that I decided I wanted company for the evening, I wanted a chat and a laugh. My own company was becoming insufferable!

I spotted a couple who turned up in the bar and it was obvious from the way they were greeted this was not their first time at the resort. They looked like they came from the UK and appeared great fun. The next night I saw them again, finished my dinner and sat at the bar beside them. Before long I had new friends; they were from Stoke but lived in Australia. I also found an Irish pub with a live band. The band were brilliant and I soon joined in with the dancing and singing. If you go alone you need to be prepared to get up and join in, either that or stay on your own for the evening, every evening! I think it also says how safe I felt that I was confident enough to do this.

However, there was a need for caution, not drinking too much and staying in public areas, making sure you are able to get back to your hotel quickly and safely. It seemed with Phuket that it was obvious where the action was and the areas to avoid, unless that was what you wanted.

Walking Street is a long pedestrianised area with bars and free sex shows, yes, the ones with the ping pong ball (allegedly I might add). It was very colourful, extremely vibrant and certainly worth a walk around just to experience it.

From Phuket I boarded a ferry to Railay, a beautiful resort only reachable by boat. It isn't an island but it is cut off from the nearby town of Krabi by huge lime rock stacks, which are impassable except by sea. A small boat took a group of us to the resort. On arriving at the resort the only way to access it was to jump off and walk to the beach in the sea. That's okay but not if you have a heavy rucksack and hand luggage. Thankfully a man took my luggage, in addition to his own, to the safety of the beach. Another example of a small act, at the right time, making such a difference to me. I have learnt to be grateful for the many small things on this trip. I have found that people notice me and will often chat to find out what I'm doing, if I am really on my own. This happened in Railay. A lovely Austrian guy chatted to me at the bar but his girlfriend got really annoyed and they had a massive fight about it!

I booked a boat trip to make the most of transportation to Krabi before heading further down south to catch a train through Malaysia to Singapore. It was during this five-island trip on the boat that my rucksack got soaked and everything in it got soaking wet. Thankfully there are laundry services everywhere and air con can be turned up high to dry out bags. It was after the soaking of the rucksack and its contents that I learnt there was a rain cover in the top pocket – you live and learn as they say!

Again, with my sodden bag now weighing heavier someone came to my rescue getting me off the boat to get to Krabi and found me a lift along the long jetty; a motorcycle ridden by a twelve-year-old boy! From the jetty a taxi was ordered to take me to Krabi.

Krabi was interesting and I spent a lovely morning with a local man on his boat going around the mangroves and sights on the river. Needless to say he probably charged me highly and I gave in to a second hour with him to see the fish farms. But I enjoyed it and he could probably now feed his family that week!

That's the bottom line out in SE Asia, my money was worth a great deal more than theirs and the little that is given to them by way of tourist trips, such as a boat ride, goes a long way. I had a lovely few hours on the river, looking at mud cleaners, which are fish that clean the mud banks of crabs and small prawns. There were also monkeys and a very large lizard.

After a few days In Krabi I boarded a local minibus and headed to Hat Yai to pick up the train to take me to Singapore. The train journey from Hat Yai to Singapore, lasting twenty-seven hours in three trains in a first class seat, costs less than £20 in total! The journey to Hat Yai was like being on an episode of *Top Gear*, it was an exciting and fast drive. The mini bus was crowded but I had a great view out of the front window behind the driver.

Hat Yai itself was closer to the border with Malaysia. It was very different from any other experience of Thailand, there was a huge Muslim presence and most of the women were dressed in the traditional hijab. It was a busy, transient old town. The hotel that I had booked was a kilometre out of the town centre and was fairly new. The tuk tuk driver found it difficult to find, even though I helped him by using google maps. His vehicle was so old and slow that at one point Google sent a message saying it was re-estimating time of arrival and added on two extra minutes!

After two days in Hat Yai I made my way to the main station and boarded a train headed for Kuala Lumpur, much to my excitement! Singapore next stop!

Singapore

I travelled from Hat Yai, Thailand, to Singapore by train. I was so excited to be travelling by train via the iconic city of Kuala Lumpur. 'Just bought a train ticket to Kuala Lumpur, how cool is that?' was my Facebook status that day.

Each train had a cleaner on board, cleaning toilets and sweeping floors. It really made a difference to the experience, as the trains were not modern but were clean and comfortable. The food on the train was diabolical, very cheap but plain awful. I had bought a picnic of snacks from Starbucks, luckily.

There were berths for sleeping in and I managed to book a lower bunk to save the embarrassment of having to climb up the side of the beds whilst the train was moving. The berth was comfortable and private. I sat and enjoyed watching Thailand change to Malaysia, surprised at how the landscape varied from country to country. In Malaysia the land was covered by mile after mile of banana and palm olive tree plantations. It looked very tropical and green.

The appearance of the people changed to Muslim dress, the biggest change, as always, was in the way the women looked. I was one of four westerners on the train, which crossed the boarder from Thailand to Malaysia.

A border control for the two countries was in the station at Pedang Besar. It was not necessary to change trains at the border but rather get off with all luggage, go through security and border control then get back on again after about a wait of an hour. I was not sure what would happen and hadn't filled out an exit slip for Thailand and had to go back and get my rucksack from the train to pass through security. Needless to say I was the last passenger through the control area.

There was an upstairs café for passengers to wait whilst the train was cleared to cross over in to Malaysia. It was in this café that I found a very helpful Malaysian family who helped me set up my phone with a new SIM card. I have been amazed by how many really helpful people I have met on this trip and here I met another group. One of the most cheering contacts with strangers was from those who enquired as to where I was going and remarking on the fact that I travelled alone. I didn't find their inquisitiveness at all nosey but rather took courage from their interest and felt less alone as a result. A smile can be so welcome when you travel alone

I experienced slight motion sickness whilst travelling so far on the train. I put it down to not eating properly. Rather than having a proper meal I was snacking. I made my way to the buffet car at midnight and ate an omelette and plain rice. On returning to my berth I switched the end for the pillow, making sure I was travelling feet first. Whether the food or change of travel direction helped, the symptoms soon subsided and I began to feel better

I arrived in Kuala Lumpur main station early the next morning and bought onward tickets to Johor Bahru in order to cross the causeway to Singapore.

I had timed my visit to Singapore to coincide with family coming to see me from the UK. It felt unusual having to time my travel to fit in with someone else's plans after going alone for so long. On arriving in Singapore I stayed at the Ibis Hotel purely for the luxury of beautiful bed linen and a comfortable bed. I booked three nights and enjoyed the relative western feel of Singapore. I watched an old time favourite film and had a glass of wine in bed. It felt like real luxury.

As on previous occasions I made a deliberate move to have some company of westerners during the evening by starting conversations myself. I laughed at myself in the bar in the Ibis as I asked a lady if she too was travelling alone. Thankfully she saved my embarrassment and was, but what amused me was when does, 'Are you travelling alone?' cease to sound like a chat up line! I can assure you it wasn't, simply a conversation starter, but it did make me wonder!

I used the few days before meeting up with family to find out what Singapore had to offer. It wasn't a place I had wished to go but was one that I found myself in to fit in with them. It is so different from any of the other countries I had been to on the way. Gone was the litter, the poverty, the dirty animals and poor children, squalid dwellings, dust roads to be replaced by a squeaky clean, highly efficient Singapore. It really felt astonishing. It is usually visited on the way to a far-flung destination, a stop off for a few days between flights.

If I had come flown in from home or Australia I may not have been so amazed by the high standards or the sharp contrast between Singapore and neighbouring Malaysia. Everything looked busy, clean, smart, happening – the metro system was cheap and easy to navigate. Rather like our Oyster card in London, one ticket did all modes of transport. The harbour area was smart, beautiful high rise buildings, and parks to walk in. There were endless shopping malls and high street shopping areas. The high-end shops were gleaming but I noticed there were not a great deal of people buying anything as Singapore is expensive, especially for this side of the world.

Singapore had been colonized by the British from 1819 to the start of the Second World War when it was captured by the Japanese. It returned to British rule in 1945. The following years saw an increase in self-government until it was merged with Malaya to form Malaysia in 1963. This was not a happy merger and ended in 1965 when Singapore became an independent republic.

From the 1960s onwards the prime minister of Singapore, Lee Kuan Yew, took Singapore from being a colonial outpost, having no natural resources to being a highly efficient and successful economy. He used his education and trade policies to unite the people, encourage them to work past individual barriers of race or creed, and ensured that the accepted language of the country was English. This helped to secure trade relations with the west.

Singapore is in an ideal place to be a trading country and resting point. It is easily reached by sea by its big exporting neighbours, like China, India and Australia. It has a large off shore space for storage and trade in addition to an excellent hotel and tourist trade for ordinary travellers. I found it fascinating. It was so different from anything else I had experienced in SE Asia and, in some way, in reminded me of home.

During my visit fifty years of remaining independent was celebrated. 'Singapore at 50' was the slogan that was on every billboard and transport ticket. I searched for evidence of the colonial times but found few. The museum only had exhibits going back fifty years, focusing on the anniversary. Eventually, I found a glimpse of the colonial past whilst visiting the famous Raffles Hotel.

This was a real treat, partly due to the cost of lunch and wine but also due to the perfectly restored past glory easily seen in the décor and exuberance. It felt very British. I had a lovely Sunday brunch there and simply soaked up the atmosphere. Having eaten off plastic plates and with cheap cutlery most of the time I really appreciated the china crockery and quality cutlery. I'm sure wine tastes nicer from a beautifully crafted glass!

I noticed a couple a few tables away from me helping themselves to the buffet and piling up their table with a selection of food. The buffet here was amazing, everything on offer from starters through to dessert. The lady of the couple came over and asked me to join them. It was a funny moment because I was actually indulging a habit of people watching and this invitation would suspend this particular enjoyment. However, I am glad I joined them. I enjoyed a mad afternoon of food, cigarettes and wine. The restaurant had closed but they were frequent visitors and were set for the afternoon. We found a shaded table outside while the dining room was being cleared and continued our conversation.

They were interested in my travels, I told them where I had been and what my plans were.

The man of the couple had connections with Singapore that drew him back for regular visits. His grandmother had been on the last boat out of the country at the onset of the Japanese invasion in the Second World War. She had been on a boat that thankfully didn't sink and reached Australia safely.

His grandfather had been one of the British soldiers who had been captured by the Japanese, he had survived his captivity but had been only five stone in weight when he was released. I had a very enjoyable and informative afternoon with them. I had looked for signs of Singapore pre-independence and I felt I had really got a sense of it from being in Raffles and talking with this couple.

Any visit to Raffles is not complete without a drink at the Long Bar, famous for its past notorious drinkers, such as Humphrey Bogart and Earnest Hemingway. Here was the birthplace of the famous 'Singapore Sling' cocktail. The drinks were overpriced but the atmosphere made up for the extra charge. The original ceiling fans were still cooling the bar and the floor was covered in peanut shells. Peanuts were available all around the bar in hessian sacks and it is tradition to crack the nuts and throw the shells on the floor.

It was in Singapore that I decided to have a medical examination. It was the first country where I had felt confident enough in their standards and not overwhelmed by language barriers. The service was efficient, my worries put quickly to rest and medication given. The only other medical attention I had needed since I left home was for ant bites I had in Cambodia. The treatment for the bites was in a back street shack behind the central market. The bites were sorted but I remember thinking at the time that I was thankful I had no serious examinations to go through.

I had been well on this trip and for that I was extremely thankful. I took care to eat fresh food and plenty of water. The one issue I had not thought about was the replacement of salt in my body. In these hot climates the body sweats in the heat and a lot of the salts are lost which are not replaced by simply drinking water. Another fact was that Asian cooking used less salt and more sugar than I was used to. I drank a rehydration sachet each time I began to feel tired or listless.

Singapore benefited from the efficiency of its public transport system. The roads do not snarl up from heavy traffic as the metro train system was cheap, safe and clean to use. As a visitor I found this very easy to use and navigate my way around the small country. In addition to this ease I began to notice that all the public signage conveyed a positive message. Messages such as, 'Work smarter – Have more time for family life', 'Go to college – Get a better job and future', were a few I noticed. It felt very different to the signage I was used to seeing in the UK where we are encouraged to claim for accidents and that the Inland Revenue or Fraud Squad is watching us!

The signs in the trains suggested, rather than demanded, that priority for seats was given to pregnant women or disabled people. It made me feel like I would be doing a good thing not simply following rules and regulations, or obligations even. There was no pushing or foul language, no groups of youths causing trouble or threatening behavior. It was all squeaky clean and orderly. My ideal vision of the UK!

The surroundings reminded me of home but the atmosphere was different. I had friends living in Singapore and on meeting up with them I asked if the clean atmosphere was really true or was I missing something? Apparently porn or corruption are severely dealt with and it is difficult to buy your way out of trouble. Even certain Internet sites or TV stations are prohibited because they are deemed unsuitable for public viewing, not conducive with the vision for Singapore. Chewing gum is banned! The message for drug traffickers is clear, 'You will be killed' it said on my entry visa slip. But how could this be? Surely the dirt had to be somewhere? We're human beings, we lead messy lives and sometimes act inappropriately or dangerously. This all seemed to be true but after several conversations with people I discovered it was possible to get things that were not allowed or have access to banned substances or whatever.

But the main feeling I felt was one of control. Elections were coming up and it would remain to be seen if Singapore continues in this way. Certain discussions with locals rendered a sense of them living oppressed lives, not truly free to be who they are, always obliged to conform. But surely some sense of conformity is required for us to lead peaceful lives? I did not see any religious tension in Singapore. Chinese, Indian, Muslim and Christians all lived with respect for each other. It was an offence to abuse or comment on another's religion.

Singapore has benefited from having a government that is not corrupt and does not allow corruption in its country. I detected a British undertone here. The prime minister who had so famously shaped this country had achieved a first class law degree from Cambridge University and had good relations with, and the respect of, our politicians. The sewage and transport system had a Victorian feel to it. The language, the traffic, the food all very British mixed with Chinese. China town was lovely, especially at night, so many places to eat and the lights are beautiful.

The Chinese occupied Singapore in the past and evidence of their dexterity is obvious from the Chinese shop houses outside the main centre. Thankfully not all of these beautiful old shop houses were torn down and replaced as part of the rebuilding of Singapore. It's an important part of their heritage as many of the generations of Chinese families remain and see themselves as being Singaporean.

I stayed in one of these old properties on the second half of my visit in an old part of Singapore on the Joo Chiat road. It was a beautiful old area, full of character with interesting small shops and eateries. The downstairs of the property had once been open for business with the business owners living upstairs. The stairway was narrow and step, the rooms cool with high ceiling and beautiful windows. A really classy property. It accommodated myself, and my visitors, very comfortably. It also meant that we did not have to pay expensive prices for hotel rooms as the prices had shot up due to the coming Grand Prix event being held in the city centre.

The visit of family was welcome, very welcome. It was exciting to go to the airport to meet them. Airports are great places to welcome people but hard places to say farewell. I watched my son and his grandfather walk away and return home. I found that very difficult. I didn't want to go with them, that was clear to me, but equally I didn't want the visit to end. We had had such a relaxed time together. We enjoyed a few days visiting the highlights of Singapore and even managed to gate crash a hotel lift to get us to the thirty-ninth floor of a famous hotel with a boat bar and restaurant on the top floor. The weather was good but very hazy so paying to get to the top floor would have been pointless as there was little to see through the smog. Apparently, Indonesia was burning forests, something that occurs each year, with the result of the neighbouring countries being covered in smog.

It was a strange experience being so far away from home yet being met by family. It took time to think through, to relax enough to enjoy the time, stop my travelling and not fret at the time speeding past, hurrying toward the ominous farewells at the airport I knew would come in a few days. A very short time. I enjoyed my son's company, catching up with him, feeling proud and frustrated with him in equal measure, he was such good company. I reminded myself that his teenage attitude had driven me to distraction at home, becoming increasingly frustrated with his long lay-ins and untidy bedroom. He had been a good version of his usual self whilst visiting me and I had ignored annoying traits, preferring to enjoy his company instead and not spoil our time together.

It was a happy sad parting. As I watched them leave I knew exactly what I had to do, go back to the flat we had stayed in, clear away after their visit and move swiftly on.

I booked in to the Ibis, where I had started my visit to Singapore, took advantage of the comfortable bedding, luxurious shower, restaurant and bar. Here I planned my journey going forward, having finished up any tears at the parting the previous evening. I was back on the trail. Onward. This whole episode confirmed to me that I was doing the right thing for me but also for them. The decision to simply walk away for a whole year was exactly what I should be doing. I had experienced bursts of guilt at leaving the kids; would they cope? In hindsight I think I did them a great service by being away, allowing them to grow up fully and take responsibility for themselves. As a family we needed space.

Malaysia, next stop!

Malaysia

Johor Bahru – Kuala Lumpur – Penang – Kuala Lumpur

Crossing the border from Singapore to Johor Bahru, Malaysia, was just like crossing the Severn Bridge to get in to Wales but with an added passport check and stamp. It was the easiest border I had crossed in SE Asia. But the difference between the immaculate standards in Singapore and those in Malaysia was very noticeable. Even the atmosphere seemed that much more gloomy and polluted.

The roads were busy, jammed with lorries and cars. I had spotted my hotel from the shuttle window and knew it was close to the station, too close to warrant the cost of a taxi, and started to walk in its direction with my rucksack on my back. Like in other places somebody stepped forward to give me directions and advice on how to get to the hotel. Incredible. The smallest of gestures can mean so much when you are travelling alone in a strange country. I could see the hotel but had to get across two busy major motorways to get it. There was no path and no other way to get across other than simply running for it. Not easy with a rucksack on my back!

The following morning I took the train to Kuala Lumpur (KL), a seven-hour trip costing thirty-three ringgits, about £4.50! Included in the price of the ticket was a bottle of water and a piece of cake, I had fallen asleep but when I awoke the train buffet service brought me my water and cake.

In KL I had booked a cheap hotel, close to the station, closer than I imagined, a two street taxi ride cost more than my train journey! But at least I got the chance to orientate myself. The second time I stayed I walked through the station complex to the hotel. The stations are incredibly busy, lots of places to eat and shop. Unfortunately, they are not air-conditioned and the main concourse can get very hot and stuffy. They are well-organized, good signage, plenty of rest rooms and toilets. The departures are easy to understand, either Gate A or B. From KL I headed up to Penang to spend a week in Georgetown. I had a week to spare before a friend joined me for the weekend in KL so I did not want to spend the whole of the time in one city.

At KL station, which was crowded, busy and hot, I noticed another female traveller, very well dressed but obviously travelling alone. It's funny how solo travellers can recognise each another without introduction. We both ended up in the first class carriage and eventually introduced ourselves. I had intended to take the ferry across to the island of Penang but she had planned a taxi. The taxi would cost around $50, whilst the ferry, including a shuttle from the train, would cost 1.20 ringgits, around 67p. We took the ferry! This was easy now as we had each other's company and we arrived on the island after ten-thirty in the evening. We were staying at separate hotels but exchanged contact details and met up a few times over the visit to enjoy a local wine bar together and a taxi tour of the island.

Georgetown was great to visit. I stayed slightly out of town, in a medium range hotel, including breakfast, with a roof top pool. It was clean, modern and popular. The walk to the main centre was about half an hour but there was a free shuttle service close by linking a large shopping centre with the old town. The island of Penang had been colonized by the British from mid-nineteenth century until the Straits Settlement after the Second World War when it became part of the Malayan Union. Independence was gained from Britain in 1957. It was briefly occupied by the Japanese during World War Two

Today it still has a legacy of transportation, language and law rather like our own in the UK. It still retains the old street names, which only add to the atmosphere of Georgetown itself. Places like *Love Walk* and *Rope Lane*, each having intricate steel sculptures which give brief information on how it got that name originally. It really was a lovely place to walk around. The old Chinese style shop buildings were full of interesting merchandise and tourist gifts.

I loved the street art. I took a guided walk to each of the building size murals created by the European artist, Ernest Zacharevic. The whole of Georgetown had a shabby-chic feeling to it. The island of Penang was a fascinating place to visit; the colonisation and rich trading history provided much interest from the wonderfully preserved town houses. These town houses had the best of everything, tiles from Italy, glass, furniture and wood shipped from all over the world. They all were symmetrical in design with a central open-air courtyard to catch much needed rain, provide light and cool the interior rooms.

My love of photography was satisfied by a visit to the camera museum. The museum glorified film and the early film cameras.

The Japanese had occupied Penang during the war and evidence of their cruel methods were apparent from a visit to the war museum, an untouched base high on a high over looking the straits of Menacca. The visit to Penang was completed by visiting the highest point, Penang Hill. I took a funicular train both up and down the hill, I didn't fancy the walk up nor back down again! The route on the train was incredibly steep but the views over Penang and over to mainland Malaysia were worth the trip. Penang is connected to the mainland by two bridges and a ferry; one of the bridges is 13.5k long. After a short, lovely week in Penang the train was full when I arrived at the station so I made my way back to KL by local bus, which cost just short of £5.

On this journey I have always had confidence in my intuition when it comes to trusting or not the people that I meet. I took a taxi on my arrival back in KL and the driver suggested a few places to visit. I had planned to visit Melaka, some three hours away by bus from KL. It was another costal town that had been occupied by the British, after the Portuguese. We discussed a price, better than going on the bus and more convenient.

But what of taking a taxi with a strange man, on my own, to a city over two hours away from KL? I could go missing and no one would be any the wiser as to where I had gone or to which direction I had taken. To minimize the risk I let a friend know where I was going and the plate number of the taxi. I told the taxi driver that I had let the hotel know the details of his cab and my expected time back that evening.

It was an interesting cab ride. We had a detailed discussion about life, love, religion, disappointment in life and Malaysia. He was a deep thinker who was also deeply disappointed in life. His first wife had died and he had married, after a nine-year stint on his own, another woman, much younger. He felt trapped and unhappy, he said he stayed for the children. He expressed an idea that had he and I had met earlier in life we would have been very happy together. He loved my smile.

There had been occasions on this trip, when I had had to rebuff the unwanted attention from men, this occasion was different, this was spoken attention and a lot of flattery. He wanted to take me to meet his wife for dinner after the trip. I can only imagine that she too felt a sense of disappointment where she had ended up with this man who did not return her love. I reluctantly agreed to call in with her, but not to eat with them.

They lived in a concrete box; that was the way I saw it. It had roller shutters and no windows, I stood under the roller shutter so it could not be brought down without me having to move. The wife was well dressed and had dressed her sons up to meet me. The whole experience was surreal. I had kept my door unlocked in the car and sat in the back seat. He asked me about this, asking if I felt unsafe. I replied that I was merely being sensible. I told him that I felt I could trust him but I was in no way interested in anything more than a visit to Malacca and chit-chat.

He was a Muslim and explained that his beliefs kept him on the straight and narrow. But he said he was a bad Muslim in his head. Although I took a risk going with him that day I have no regrets, I had a very interesting insight in to the thinking of a man from Malaysia and their culture behind closed doors.

I spent a few days in KL waiting for the arrival of a friend from the UK. I used the time to have a look around Chinatown and booked to have dinner in a 'Dining In The Dark' experience. This restaurant was run by partially-sighted people with the dining area in pitch darkness. I could not see my hand in front of my face. I was led to my seat by keeping my hand on the shoulder of someone just literally a step in front of me, guided to a chair and briefed about the things on the table in front of me. The only food option was a set menu and afterwards I was asked to guess what I had eaten.

I was aware of other guests in the room, but I could not tell you the size of the room or anything about any of the other people around me. Being on my own I was able to concentrate and simply listen. My food arrived and the waiter explained where everything was and the order in which I should eat it. My sense of hearing was acute, I worked out how the waiters communicated their movements to each other by a clicking of their tongues. But I could not taste anything and I did not finish my food as I could not judge how much I had eaten or what it was. At the end of the meal my partially-sighted host sat at the table and we had an interesting discussion on my experience and what it was like to be blind.

I learnt that blind people like to be independent but do require certain clues from sighted people to enable them to navigate their way around. Needless to say I guessed the menu wrongly as I was relying totally on touch and taste, sight is so important to whole enjoyment of food.

My friend arrived and we enjoyed the opulence of the Traders Hotel with a splendid view of the Petronas Towers from our window. The Traders has a lovely sky bar, with great music and views of the city; also expensive drinks to match! But this was a treat, a celebration of meeting up again. The visit ended with a trip to the top of the Petronas Towers for incredible views of the city, really worth a visit.

I had made my mind up to cease travelling after KL and I booked a plane to Cambodia to volunteer for a further two weeks in Hope School and revisit the lovely Cambodian guide and his family I had spent time with earlier in the year. I had enjoyed Malaysia but on returning to Cambodia and being in a tuk tuk going through the incredibly busy streets of Phnom Penh I felt real pleasure again at everything I saw. I was glad to be back.

I realised I had lost the bug to travel, I was no longer overwhelmed by wonder of being in new places as I had been. Maybe meeting up with family members had brought me back down to earth or having spent time in KL with a close friend had taken the edge off, I'm not sure. Or maybe it was because Malaysia was covered in white smoke from the forestry fires in Indonesia, an annual problem apparently. Regardless, I knew I had to do something and it certainly wasn't to go home.

I had been offered a place in a school in Thailand to help teach English but that wasn't starting until a couple of months after this time in Malaysia. I decided to fly to Cambodia from KL and return to the school that I had originally volunteered at. I would then travel on to Seam Reip across the Tonle Sap Lake by boat and revisit the guide whose company I had enjoyed at the start of my trip.

This was a great idea from one point, I was able to think through some lesson plans for Thailand and gather some teaching resources. However, the living standards at the project had gone downhill somewhat and, in addition to this, it was badly supervised. There was no cook and the hygiene standards were dreadful. It was a long two weeks of noodles and cleaning but I made another set of lifelong friends. Thankfully I had been given two large jars of marmite, which fed both me and another volunteer for two weeks.

Again, there was the same sense of community that I had encountered on my first stint, which is the up side of volunteering and living as a group like this, you really bond with people, especially if you become one of the 'mummy' ones and go to the market to get food to prepare a decent meal!

Teaching English Abroad – Volunteering In Cambodia

Hope School is situated in Angtasoam, which is two hours south of Phnom Penh, in rural farming, among poor villages. It was a difficult experience but one that I would not have missed, in fact I even went back to do a further fortnight before settling in Thailand to teach for a while. It was primitive, beautiful, attended by heart crushingly beautiful, poor children.

Again, it was obvious to me how hard women work in these parts of the world. Up early in the morning, childcare, going to buy or sell produce at the market, cooking, tending to the livestock. The village had small 'shops' in front of the houses, selling snacks, beer, spirits, local meat and vegetables, taking in laundry, all run by the women and children. Just behind the shelving you could see the family home with TV and sleeping pallets. There were normally cows and chickens loose in the yard.

The shocking reality was that despite the poor conditions of the houses and roads in the villages the temples were resplendent and beautifully maintained. Inside each one were beautifully tiled flooring and paintings depicting the stories and lives of Buddha. Each day the monks would be fed from the village people bringing hot dishes and rice.

An early morning walk to the temple provided an interesting insight into the life of the village and the place the temple provided. Another volunteer and I discovered the entire village gathered before the monks. Each family was seated together, with baskets of food for the monks and then for themselves. Needless to say they were delighted to see us and invited us to sit down with them. There followed the usual round of us being given babies to hold and our skin touched, or rather pinched.

The school in Cambodia was open Monday to Friday 1.30 p.m. to 6.00 p.m. Groups of children attended for an hour each day, according to age and ability. Despite being totally run by volunteers it was quite well organised from a teaching point of view despite the accommodation for the volunteers being primitive.

Some of the basic needs were ignored, like access to fresh food and a secure sleeping area. We slept in bunk beds in a metal clad dorm. I was awoken one evening by sparks coming from a live wire hanging down the wall beside a mosquito net over a bunk. I lay awake, checking at intervals for signs of a fire starting on the net of my sleeping fellow volunteer. The next morning I reported the problem, the wired was taped over, problem solved. It was incredibly hot and the ceiling fans were noisy and ineffective. It was impossible to sleep. The volunteer kitchen and shared sitting areas were filthy, flies all over the kitchen and open waste bins. I realised I was helping in a poor area but I think a few lids with bins and putting food away safely are a basic requirement.

As volunteers we were left to do chores and feed ourselves. The camp coordinator would cook once a day, when he was around, after loosing his cook to an accountancy course. We were very hungry and demoralised. But the kids made up for all the hardship and a good sense of community developed among the volunteers.

The volunteers were mainly teenagers or young adults, straight from university, taking a gap year, some mid- twenties on career breaks before settling down and then there were us older women who tended to act like mums to younger ones in the group. At weekends the group would travel together, squashed in a mini bus to relax somewhere, usually with on a beach. Despite being badly run this project was showing some success. The children were learning and beginning to speak English.

It was here that I began to toy with the idea of staying in SE Asia and teaching English. I loved Cambodia, I loved the teaching and the kids, I was sure I would get used to the conditions and that eventually things would stop biting me. There was little entertainment at the project but we entertained ourselves and regularly had beer o'clock in a local shop, sitting on plastic chairs in the front area of their house/shop. The choice was beer or Cambodian spirits, I chose beer. I would have loved to have found wine available locally but this was not to be.

The children were being taught the mechanics of the English language, verbs, nouns, adjectives, superlative and comparative adjectives. Funnily enough, I had to look up what we were teaching as I certainly didn't remember it from my school days! The children were diligent at learning English, understanding how to structure a sentence properly, the tenses, verbs, adjectives and nouns. This was in sheer contrast to what I found in Thailand. Their vocabulary was extensive.

The local school was attended in the morning for other lessons. There was a resource library, which because no one was responsible for it, was a total mess. There was a good variety of reading material and course books. During my first week I organized the books in to age category and collected all the resources that had been left around in classrooms all over the place. No one really cared about these valuable resources.

As I tackled one of the shelves I noticed a pink and green leg on the wall of the room and taking more books off the shelf to tidy and clean, came face-to-face with a very large gecko. Both of us were alarmed by the sight of the other and the gecko ran for cover. All throughout Asia geckos can be heard and seen. But this encounter had been on my first day! I became used to living with them over time but the large ones are very scary but totally harmless.

I did come across big spiders and a poisonous centipede. One of the volunteers was bitten by a poisonous snake and needed an antidote for the venom. The worse that happened to me was standing on a nest of angry red ants and being bitten, who could blame them?

The time came to leave Cambodia and move on. I would have loved to support one family of girls who were particularly smart and whose success would have made a great impact for their family. But I was unsure of how to do this and did not feel comfortable enough to know that the money would reach them. To volunteer and work with them was the best I could do for them. I have a batch of letters written to thank me and will treasure them, and the memories of their writers, forever.

Teaching Abroad – A Position In A Private School

I took up a teaching post in Thailand from November to February, working in a small rural school in the village of Bua Lai, close to the larger town of Bua Yai, five hours outside Bangkok toward the border with Laos. This was an old part of the original Thailand and, rice was the main produce out here, with each village having its own rice machine. Every morning I would set out to ride the short journey to school on my moped, passing cows, water buffalo and rice fields, dodging patchy work carried out on roads and the odd chicken that flew across in front of my path. I loved it.

I was fortunate to be able to stay with a Thai family. For the first time in seven months I could unpack my rucksack and settle for a while. I had my own room downstairs but outside my window, within a couple of feet, slept the neighbour's cows and chickens. When the sun set at around five or six that was the end of the day, nothing to do but retire to bed and read. I began to alter my routine, to get up and go to sleep with the rising or setting of the sun.

I picked up a selection of English grammar books from the local bookshop in Tesco. I prepared to compile worksheets teaching nouns, adjectives, etc., like the sentence structure we were teaching in Cambodia. I was amazed to discover that this was not the state of affairs in Thailand; in Thailand all they wanted from English was to learn how to speak it. I found this challenging, how could I teach a language without teaching the structure and vocabulary that is so essential. English is a beautiful language, one that has rules and peculiarities that need understanding to be able to use it to its full potential. This is the language of poets and an excellent match for music. Thai is a tonal language, one with endless vowels and consonants, with long sounds and short sounds changing the meaning of words. The desire for English was solely to be able to get better jobs in English speaking parts of the world.

I started in the school and asked for the text books that were being used to teach English so that I knew what was on the syllabus. These were extremely basic. I had free rein to introduce all types of ways of teaching, singing, colouring in, flash cards, games, balloons. In many ways it was exciting until I realised that I was meant to teach English without any assistance or the services of an interpreter. The task seemed impossible, even the teachers had no English.

I was on my own. Any amount of grammar books whereas not going to be an ounce of help! In some classes I was left alone to manage large groups of twenty- five plus kids. I made sure that in preparation for classes I had some basic sentences or commands to control the class and communicate with any teaching staff. It became evident that I had to learn such phrases as 'Sit down', 'Listen', 'Say with me' and 'What is this?' My Thai, although a bit messy, improved very quickly and I kept a set of written phrases to use at a moments notice, such as 'What is this?'

I made some bi-lingual signs that I could use to quickly communicate with teachers, getting their assistance to convey instructions. At times when no teacher was present I simply worked out who was the smartest and most compliant pupil in the class, usually a girl, show them a sign and ask them to give instruction to the class. This worked and in a funny way aided their learning, after a week of using the signs and my basic Thai the class started to say the words back to me in English. It was something of a small miracle.

Eventually the school gave me a schedule to work to and the use of an interpreter most of the time. But there was a great deal of work to do. However, you can't rush kids, especially in Thailand, and I had to continue at their pace. It worked out well. The appreciation and welcome I received each day made up for the sleepless nights I spent panicking about how to make it work.

I had to find a way to provide opportunity for my pupils to talk, to speak English independently. They were very confident at shouting responses learnt like parrots as a whole class but I wanted to encourage conversation. But how, surely they needed vocabulary first? I used flash cards, which were very useful, and finger puppets to try to get them to talk individually and at the same time engage a whole class. I began to use flash card games of my own making. Resources were difficult to come by. I discovered, no great surprise I guess, that they responded enthusiastically to games, team games and loved competition.

Board games can be too small to be enjoyed by a whole class so I began to assemble laminated 'squares' set up like a board, which could be laid out on a large table or floor. A dice was used in the usual way to take turns and make moves, plastic animals were used as counters. I interspersed the flash cards they were familiar with alongside instructions to spell or ask a question, perform an action, written on the card to introduce verbs. The children were divided in to smaller teams of three to four, each team would have to read the instruction for their team and do the task required. Fun, and it worked, they began to speak to each other in English, with the aid and support from myself. The school had a translator and I insisted that he helped me with the older classes.

A second option I explored was the possibility of teaching English at home in the village. Children came on weekends to practice spoken English. A major problem, and source of great hilarity, was pronunciation. The sessions were fun but whilst everyone raved about it in the beginning the numbers began to dwindle as the novelty wore off. It was also difficult to prepare for and teach appropriate language skills as the group dynamics were changing all the time with students coming and going. It was hard to pitch the level right and when I did find the level the group would change again. I now work with individuals simply working on pronunciation and conversation skills. It's much easier.

The outcome of the teaching was positive as in the end the school wanted me to stay on another year as the kids were so fond of me and we were making progress despite the language barriers. The translator I had sporadically left the school and I was left to continue unaided. The teachers became less wary of me as time passed and each one purchased an English book to enable them to communicate with me, at the same time I brushed up on my Thai. I was invited to the staff New Year's party and enjoyed their company very much, karaoke has no language barriers and with the help of good food, a half-decent stereo system and Spy Wine an enjoyable night was had by all.

I became more settled in the school, began to enjoy the experience and reverted to having a good night's sleep once more. It became less of an issue that I was the only English speaker and did not have a translator to help during lessons. Once it was clear that this was the way it would be it became less of a problem, I simply needed to account for this during preparation for lessons. I did this by using bi-lingual flash cards and books, which enabled me to work with class teachers. Also Google was useful in finding simple translations for using the white board.

I made sure I knew how to ask questions in Thai, such as 'What colour is this?' or 'How many?' etc. I used the younger children to teach me how to count, days of the week, months of the year, colours, in Thai, which they enjoyed immensely. I really believe this approach added to their enjoyment of learning English. They delighted in correcting my pronunciation as I corrected theirs. Being the only English speaker made the task a challenge but it was not insurmountable. I insisted in having a Thai teacher with me. Preparations for teaching had to include ways of communicating with these teachers.

I have found the children learn effectively through singing and action songs. To this end I had to develop my singing voice and get over any shyness for singing in public or in front of a class, even leading two classes using a microphone for the school concert in front of parents. Who would have thought it!

Teaching in this environment presented a problem on a personal level as I never felt part of the teaching team. I was not invited to attend staff meetings as I would not understand what was being discussed. The quicker I learnt basic Thai the better. The master of the school had a daughter studying in Bangkok who spoke English. I was able to converse with her and then for her to relay messages back and forward from her father to me.

School events or holidays would happen and I would be unaware of any changes and, prepare for lessons to find that that was unnecessary or have to deliver something in a shorter time than planned. Everybody, but me, seemed to know what was happening. Thankfully there were a few Thai/English speakers I could call on to help with this issue. In Thailand there are something like thirty-eight days holiday in school time, Buddha days, the king's birthday, Mother's Day for the queen. I began to feel upset by this lack of inclusion. It felt as if I was making every effort to bridge the language gap to enable me to teach English but this effort was not returned.

On celebration or holiday days, children are paraded in Thai national costume, excessive make-up, looking like dolls. Even the boys wore rouge or lip stick with their traditional costumes. Dressing up, dancing and performing was greatly enjoyed by all and became an opportunity to showcase the school. Sports Day started with an elaborate parade from a local house, complete with fully dressed up kids and marching band. Despite this grand opening the actual sports events were only a few races, a tug-of-war and a ball game. Nevertheless, enjoyed by all.

Despite all the difficulties thrown up by the language barrier I was successful at teaching four classes some English. The two kindergarten classes had four English lessons per week, per class. At first I saw this as a bit of a waste of time but in reality it provided a perfect opportunity to teach the basics – the alphabet, colours, body parts, numbers, days of the week, months, animals, etc. I introduced a very simple form of the verb 'to be' in the present tense only. This was not a waste of time with these younger ones and I am certain the earlier they begin to learn the better, sooner seemed an excellent time to start.

It was at this point I decided that I would like to find out if this early foundation teaching was reaping benefits. I thought about teaching for an entire school year. This age group are fun to teach, using songs, poems and colouring in of work sheets. They loved books and stories. I found some books in the local supermarket that had both Thai and English on the same page. This enabled the teacher and I to read the story to the class together. The primary classes I had two lessons per class per week. In one way this was not long enough. However, compared to most schools, who allow one hour per week to English, this was a good start.

Both the primary classes had English books to follow but like most resources they had a very American feel and spelling. They did provide a type of syllabus to follow. I used the content of the books, Smile 1 and 2, to construct a curriculum to follow in the kindergarten years. I added simple sentences when teaching from the Smile books. One thing I have observed is that written English is working here although spoken English is problematic. There appeared to be a total lack of comprehension on how the tenses or singular/plurals work or the importance of punctuation. Thai and English do not translate easily as both languages work in different ways.

Google translate is hilarious! There was no understanding of how a sentence works. How could there be when different rules apply. Even the formation and placing of letters is totally different. I had to go back to basics.

My intention was to make some kind of a guide for myself and the other teachers to follow. Any session plans were then translated for me in to Thai. I started by encouraging simple sentence structure, vocabulary and correct use of the tenses. Pronunciation was another area to work on. Sounds of words, especially those containing th, v, r, or s, had to be broken down and each sound pronounced separately. Tongue twisters were great fun to practice saying words. I enjoyed the time with this school immensely. The children were so loving and rewarding.

The end of the school year came in February. There were tests to be taken. I was asked to set a test for the primary school children, six questions, thirty points in total.

The last English exam the pupils had previously taken every single one of them had failed. Without any consultation with me the translator, who had left rather abruptly, had downloaded a paper from the internet. I had no idea about the test until it arrived one day. I saw the paper and was horrified. Nothing in the paper had been covered in the lessons. I set the exam this time to test what I had taught the children since starting. These were eight-year-olds. The test was set in English. I was so worried – what if they failed this time?

Thankfully every student was successful in passing and there was a good spread of those who had done well and those who had done well enough to pass. It was a good end to the year for me, and the pupils were delighted too.

I was approached by the senior school to run an English course. I agreed to give it a try but was clear that I wished to remain loyal to the junior school. I was able to fit the course in around my schedule. I was assured that there was no work to do, no preparation, just simply talk with the students. I arrived to find that there were in fact three groups of students and no preparation had been made to run a session. I was asked to sing, 'The Wheels on the Bus' with these students who were in their upper teens.

I decided at that moment that I would prepare my own sessions to include reading, singing and discussion. These students were fun, eager to learn and incredibly well mannered. I enjoyed working with them and the work was relatively easy. This is an age group I intend to work with more in the future but for now my time in Asia was drawing to an end and it was nearly time to go home.

I loved the experience of teaching English in both the Cambodian and Thai schools. In both countries the children are polite, diligent and eager to learn. To speak English and speak it well would mean better prospects for jobs in the future. There is no employment on the family farms or in the rural communities. As tourism grows in these developing countries it is essential that efforts are made to prepare the local people to have a major role in the work force.

Missing Friends and Family

Thai villages, away from the better known tourist areas, are sleepy and quiet. Quiet that was until someone in the family died then it was loud music from early morning until the early hours, loud bangs and monks chanting to send the deceased's spirit on its way. The Thais are incredibly superstitious.

I had my room and lived as one of the family. Family was an extended affair, it usually consisted of grandparents, nephews, aunties, uncles, grandchildren, all living together. The only way to find work was to work in the factories in Bangkok, usually meaning that both parents leave, leaving babies to be brought up by grandparents

I was happy, glad to have the work to do in the local school to occupy me. There was nothing to do but read, sleep, eat, walk and think. Nothing ever happened. It took me a while to get used to having no pressure on my time, having time to myself after travelling was a real treat.

I took the time to reflect but also to think – what do you want to do next? I knew this year had changed me, extracted me from the demands of normality. It felt like a gift. However, there were times when I questioned myself about what I was doing with my life. I didn't feel homesick but I did feel lonely. I needed to be able to converse in English. I missed my friends. I made a conscious effort to enjoy this last reprieve before ending my year with the trip to Australia.

Being in a new environment had my senses working overtime, different smells, different light, unusual sights, delicious new tastes. A total treat enjoyed by all the senses. Even sounds that surrounded me were new and exciting, I took in each one. Animal noises and regular loud clanks from passing rice trucks and machines, distant booms from neighbouring villages announcing a death. It seemed the Thais had a noise for everything and every occasion. Yet somewhere along the line I missed those who knew me best and familiar surroundings. It's great to get away, to have this opportunity of a year out, but it was a long time to be away from close friends and family.

I missed a good chat with good friends that knew me, the sort of conversation that would start easily, many shared and accepted things about each other providing an enjoyable conversation, one that did not need introduction, so many things so easily understood, a shared history, a common ground, a shared joke. I began to crave the American show *Sex and the City* whose main characters are women who enjoy a close, supportive relationship with one another.

Conversing with new friends, especially those from a different culture, required new language, understanding and explanation, not a great deal of common ground, but interesting all the same. It was just different and required thought, acceptance and appreciation. It sometimes made me feel lonely or isolated, just as it can be liberating allowing me to observe without being required to join in. I needed to reconnect.

I used social media a great deal to maintain friendships from home. Social media was a strange vehicle, in its own way it can be very useful for maintaining old friendships and developing new ones. I hesitated at first to put up pictures but was encouraged by Facebook friends to keep posting as they were enjoying them and saw this as a way to follow me. Some friends are opposed to Facebook, not trusting it or liking the apparent transparency effect on their lives. Other friends, I thought would follow me or comment, totally ignored me and contacted very seldom. New friendships were forged through comments and messages.

Additionally, social media enabled these new friendships to develop and future meet ups were organised. I had a circle, a support group of friends, to whom I could simply express myself honestly, when things were bad; I had the space and permission to say so. I kept in contact with these friends by email or Facetime. It was possible to keep in touch. With my support group of friends and family I did not have to be constantly enjoying myself or appreciating the break I had taken for myself, although that went without saying. The problem with social media can be that there can appear an artificial gloss on everything, everything shiny and rosy when sometimes I just wanted to say how much I missed everyone.

But I did not feel homesick, not once, not even when I received reports from the property management company did I pine for my house with its new kitchen and bath. I missed having a bath! I loved being away, travelling and staying in foreign countries, I did not miss home. But I missed my family and close friends, especially my girl friends.

Christmas and New Year Away From Home

There are certain times when being away from home can feel more poignant, a clear tugging of familiar heart strings and traditions, knowing that you will miss out on the usual activity. I mentioned my birthday in a previous section, how isolated I felt and frankly quite spoilt. Christmas was quite a different event. There was Christmas songs and seasonal offers in the local Tesco superstore, endless choruses of 'We wish you a merry Christmas' and tinsel although Christmas is not celebrated in Thailand. New Year was the bigger event. It was a refreshing experience to shop and not to become overwhelmingly pressurised into buying items that I don't want and, worse, won't use. Nuts in shells left forever in a bowl for everyone to help themselves to immediately springs to mind as an example of this! I purchased small gifts for friends I would be staying with and the teachers at school, just small tokens.

I didn't miss having to wrap numerous parcels. I made Christmas cards, which I printed locally, and sent home. Needless to say they did not get to the UK in time for the big day! I did mourn the absence of two items and these were sprouts and crackers. The missing of Christmas crackers was the funniest as what was it about them that I missed? The hat, the joke? It just felt incomplete without seeing Christmas crackers. I organized a tree, a rather scarce outside plant, which I covered in spray snow and strung lights from. So the scene was set. But it was Christmas crackers I really missed!

I rode to school through rural countryside in blazing hot sunshine on Christmas morning. This was very different from my normal experience of Christmas in the retail trade where December is a long, hard slog running right the way up to late Christmas Eve. I was used to working hard and enjoying the buzz. As I rode past water buffalo and cows I kept reminding myself that it was Christmas Day and how different this was.

Imagine my surprise when I arrived at school to find the entire school decked in little red Santa hats and a decorated tree. I was called forward and received a present from the school, nicely wrapped in Christmas paper. It was a very humbling and thrilling experience. I'm not comfortable being the centre of attention so when the microphone was handed to me I found it hard to put together a sensible sentence or even respond properly to their generous gesture. I was quite emotional.

I had been careful to be respectful of their Buddhist beliefs during the week leading up to the event. I had produced cards to be coloured in by the children. We made Christmas trees from green cardboard and tinsel to decorate the classrooms. The class groups really enjoyed a game of 'Pass the Parcel' to tell about the act of giving wrapped presents, but how do you explain a man in a red suit who brings the packages by a reindeer drawn sleigh and puts them down the chimney? It was incredible to realise that these kids had no expectation or demand for expensive Christmas presents. They were delighted with the small packet of sweets the winner of the game won, but more than that, they were happy to line up and share the winnings.

And snowmen? I realized that 'Jingle Bells' was being sung but there was no comprehension as to what they were singing about, the words becoming muddled and meaningless. I showed them a picture of a horse drawn sleigh I downloaded from Google. Regardless, the children enjoyed the singing and the impromptu Christmas party, especially as sweets and crisps were handed out by a rather small Santa!

New Year is the main event out here. One thing that I have noted about the Thai people is that any excuse for a party is openly welcomed. They are communal people who like to work together, eat together and sit together cross-legged to watch the world go by. New Year was a four-day holiday for the entire country. The roads were rammed with thousands of people travelling back from factories in Bangkok to their home villages. There is no work locally, even though living is cheap and families stay together, young people relocate to find work.

As I wrote this chapter I was surrounded by very loud Thai music, booming out of the oversized speakers in the centre point of the village. The sun was shining, it was nine a.m. and already I could feel the mounting excitement and preparation to welcome in the New Year. Thankfully there was a cool breeze and the wind chimes did much to settle me. The evening came and went, in came the New Year. The village air was filled with the music from the enormous speakers set up at the meeting point for the village. I sat and pondered about the coming year. New Year always encourages me to reflect on the previous year and think about the next.

Village Life

Living as part of this Thai community was a beautiful way to live. Everything was so simple. Yet life was hard. They are dependent on their rice yield to feed themselves and bring in some extra cash. Each village seemed to work and support itself alongside each other. Motorbikes are shared along with the care of children and animals. The heaviest traffic can be the herds of cows or water buffaloes being walked to the now cut rice fields to feed. Food was shared among families and it was not unusual to walk past groups of people eating together.

They eat everything! Bugs, frogs, chicken feet, pigs' ears, and the beauty of their diet was that, in the main, it was self-sufficient or could be purchased very cheaply at the local weekly markets. There was a huge variety of vegetables mixed in with meat and served with copious amounts of steamed or sticky rice.

Something that I didn't realise was that, like the dogs, people are wormed too; myself now was likely to be included. I guess it made sense, everything was eaten straight out of the field or off the market stall. No pesticides are used, everything natural.

Every kitchen has a rice maker, which is put on first thing in the morning to provide the staple diet for the family and the dogs for the day. Nothing was wasted. Well-known brands of dog food would not do very well out here, the dogs are all fed on leftovers from the family's meals at the end of each day. In addition to the leftovers for the dogs were the titbits from the noodle stalls, including the chicken bones.

The population of the village was a mix of the older generation with school aged children and babies. It was the way they have to do things. The people themselves are either loud or quiet, on or off, sleeping or eating, there did not appear to be a happy medium. On passing each others' houses or visiting they simply shout to announce their arrival or passing. They are curious, kind, calm people. Everyone rode a bike, sometimes entire families rode on bikes together and no one walked anywhere!

Each village had a central meeting point that was used by the community for all sorts of things. There was also a village tuk tuk and a rice shacking machine. Their lives really were simple and shared. The mayor announced government policy changes via loud speakers and collective loans that have been granted. He seemed to be a vital link, giving information and listening to citizens needs appeared to be an important form of communication link throughout the country.

There were mosquitoes around and normal precautions of burning a repellent and applying spray to exposed skin was necessary. But the government took steps in the control of mosquitos after an outbreak of dengue fever in previous wet seasons. Their method appeared somewhat spurious. Once a year a gang of workers came and smoke bombed each house, literally you need to get out and run for cover. I was a bit bemused as to how effective this approach would be as it seemed a bit hit and miss to me.

And don't get me started on road repairs! There are two ways to get the larger village of Bua Yai a couple of miles away. One is on a lovely straight, smooth road, the other is a back road through other villages and was full of pot holes, loose gravel and crumbling road edges. Which one was 'repaired' when the money came out for road maintenance? The perfectly smooth one, of course! After a couple of weeks of the road gangs working on the road surface the perfectly smooth road became like a patchwork quilt, smooth then bumpy, smooth then bumpy. The patches got progressively smaller as the day's load of cement dwindled. The back road remained perilously crumbling with an increasing number of potholes and hidden dangers.

The village was about a mile from the main drag of the Motorway 2, which stretched between Bangkok and the northeast border with Laos. This was a section of road that was built by the Americans to enable access to Laos during the Vietnam War. What remained was a very busy, bumpy road, and like the road repair comments previously, full of potholes and bad repair jobs. You select your lane by what appears to be the less potholed section and then chance your luck with others drivers doing the same thing, eager to get past you. It was permissible to overtake on the inside as well as the outside lane. At busy times the crossroad access to the village was closed to prevent accidents from even heavier traffic and fast driving.

It was not easy to get anywhere quickly here and I preferred to take the bus or train when heading back to the civilization of Bangkok. Locally it was very easy and pleasurable to drive a scooter, with no helmet, what would my mother say? Talking of bikes, as in other East Asian countries, bikes are usually loaded up with entire families or groups of three or more. There are nasty accidents but these are less so in the rural area where I was living. Thais are a danger to themselves in that they drive fast, do not adhere to road rules or lanes and can sometimes be 'whiskied up'! Such is the relaxed atmosphere of the village life.

There appeared to be no opening or closing times, apart from the hours in which you can buy wine in Tesco! They open their business and close them as suits them. Sometimes I have walked into shops leaving without buying anything as the entire staff were asleep on hammocks or on the floor. The busiest day of the year, everyone partying, the local beauty salon was closed as the owner was playing cards! Playing cards was another thing out here, they are not allowed to play cards – it was against the law, it's gambling! So what do they do? They play cards in card schools in back rooms together, gambling for 20 baht a game. If the police come they simply pay the fine and carry on, who can blame them, what harm are they doing?

This was another example of the dichotomy that I found Thailand to be. It had strict laws regarding pornography and gambling yet both those pleasures underpin a good deal of its tourism and economy. Of course people come to visit Thailand for its natural beauty and friendliness but it was no secret as to what is available here. And speaking of the law, it's possible to buy your way out of anything. Unfortunately this leads to gross unfairness and less fortunate people feeling the weight of the system. It's human nature...

Most of the villages have their own temple and monks. The monks are central to village life. The people are very superstitious. They feed the monks to bring good luck to themselves or to send a family spirit on its way after death. The monks have no income themselves and are dependent on the people for food and everyday provisions, but there were satellite dishes outside the monks' residences and their own mobile 'phones... Most houses and businesses have shrines for Buddha into which they put flowers, food or water. Everything was blessed by the monks for 'lucky lucky', like cars, bikes or houses, etc. Monks are invited to all sorts of ceremonies and they chant in a Bali language in an unforgettable, almost calming way. They are important to this society.

On one Saturday towards the end of my stay in the village there was a celebration, for what I cannot recall because there was always a celebration of some kind going on around us. The entire village was assembled in the temple. There were a number of visiting monks, who told Buddhist stories in amusing voices, a sort of combination of chant, singing and general vocal play. It was hilarious and even though I did not understand what they were chanting it was funny. The atmosphere was light and heart-warming, entertaining to watch and be part of. I stood in the temple, amongst the people gathered together, sharing food. Everyone contributes to these occasions and eats for free, as much as you like and what you like. Most brought produce from their gardens such as corn, mango, banana, jackfruit or things that had been prepared at home. Most of the dishes were brought in baskets, which again they had made by weaving the dry grasses. My friends and I had clubbed together to buy two huge cylinders of ice cream, wafers and toppings. This probably added to our welcome!

This was another occasion when I stood and thought about the absurdity of this part of the world. Where else could you buy ice cream for an entire village on a Saturday morning and throw sticky rice balls at the monks? Needless to say these rice balls were stuffed with 20 baht notes… After the monks had been fed and showered with sticky rice, which is done apparently to give thanks for the annual yield of rice, there was a rice fight between everyone gathered. Of course, I became a prime target.

Preparing To Return Home

I spent the last week of my time in SE Asia in the mad bustling city of Bangkok. Anyone who has ever visited this city will know how cramped and busy it is – remember the song from the 80s? *One Night In Bangkok*? I was taking time to reflect and shop, ready to meet friends in Australia before flying back to the UK from Sydney a month later.

I sorely missed my friends and family, people who knew me; people to chat to and get support from. Social media was great but nothing can replace a really good chat, not even *Sex and the City*! Friends came over from the UK to join me in Bangkok for three days before they travelled on. I was so looking forward to seeing them.

It was a disaster. Travel and foreign places do not suit everyone. I had hoped for a celebration, a good ending to my time here but actually the opposite happened. I am not going to go into details but just felt it appropriate to say – watch who you travel with! Some people attract bad energy and everything goes wrong. Time will tell if we remain friends.

I felt a mixture of feelings. Time passed so quickly, what had felt like a long trip in the beginning was rapidly coming to a close. I began to find myself lamenting this and made a real effort to stop thinking about the trip coming to a close but rather enjoy the time that was left. This was a good decision. I turfed out my backpack once again, refusing to carry anything that I did not like or need. The thought of a heavily laden backpack had prevented me from impulse purchasing and carrying a load of unwanted items home. I said farewell to my friends from Nong Wa and headed to Australia via Bangkok.

In Bangkok I headed to a sky bar that I always visit. It was the place I had sat at the start of the trip when I arrived in Bangkok, tired, jet lagged, excited and asking myself 'What have I done?' as I watched the sun go down on the city. It has become a favourite view of mine as it provided an excellent place to sit and reflect, and, of course to enjoy a glass of wine or two. After a couple of visits the staff became very friendly with me, remembering that I was teaching English and practicing their pronunciation with me. Most of the people I have met have been curious about me, surprised at my decision to travel alone. I have enjoyed many discussions, meals, drinks, walks but it was a real pleasure to feel really at home in a bar so far from home.

I kept a diary of the journey and worked on putting this book together along the way. I used this time to re-read and edit what I had produced. I had to write one last chapter, Home. I wanted to write this fresh, when I arrive and settle down again. What would it feel like? Would anybody meet me at the airport? That first moment walking back to rejoin my work colleagues, seeing the kids again, walking into familiar places, catching up with friends. I had so much to tell everybody where could I possibly begin?

I remember being surprised at my feelings as I left the previous April. I thought I would be really excited after all the preparations had been completed. But I found that I wasn't excited until I sat on the plane on the runway at Heathrow airport. I think I had cried at every farewell meeting and felt numb as the day arrived to leave. I began to wait for the panic but I simply felt numb. I didn't feel scared, I felt nothing. I can remember having a lift to the station, I didn't want to be taken to the airport as I couldn't face the airport farewell. I didn't feel any regret at my decision or concern. I had simply lifted my bag and walked forward.

As the day of departure drew near I began to think about the reunion with friends and family. The return to sort out the business and other necessary arrangements like a visit to the dentist, doctor and for the obligatory over fifties trip to the breast clinic for a mammogram. Yes, things were really looking up! My daughter sent regular update messages of how long I had left, I had really felt bad about leaving her but she had done very well by herself. Social media made the world feel a much smaller place, it had been so easy to remain in touch. One family member had become ill and had failing health, but that would have happened if I had not come away. I did battle with feelings of guilt but I had spent so many years at home as a single mum that I really believed that it was my time. And it was. I know for some this will be a hard fact to come to terms with, but for me, it was absolutely clear. This was my time, I had earned it.

I saw this trip as having two endings. Firstly, the leaving of SE Asia and secondly, returning to the UK from Sydney. I had decided, on a whim, to spend the last month in Australia. I was delighted to be joined for two weeks by a friend and catch up with other friends in Sydney and Melbourne. It felt like a tidy ending. A time to head back to the vaguely familiar western feel of Australia, our distant cousins the other side of the world.

Being in Sydney was simply amazing. I felt as if I had landed back in Europe. I hadn't seen so many westerners in a long time. As I stood waiting to meet friends outside Circular Quay I noticed two things. Firstly, that it was raining and that this type of rain was cold, penetrating and unlike the rain of SE Asia which can be extremely heavy, much needed but soon over, bringing temporary relief from searing temperatures and much needed water for the vegetation.

The second thing that really struck me was when I was watching two families deal with demanding and whining children. All the children I had seen in SE Asia had very little in material things and seemed to be better off for it. The children on Circular Quay were demanding and very vocal, their parents losing the battle of control. It was a scene familiar but not missed, also a scene that I probably would not ordinarily have taken much notice. It felt funny to meet up with friends, like the closing of the year and I had to remind myself that I had Australia to come. This was something different and really planned as a treat to round up the year.

It's funny how time can seem to be endless and yet when the end comes, or was in sight, the time seemed to have flown past. I'm sure it was just as strange for my friends as we quickly caught up but it became obvious how much I had not been present for.

Being in Australia for the final month provided me with an excellent opportunity to take a breath before heading back to the UK. There's nothing that much different in Australia than the UK, apart from the numerous dangerous insects and creatures that can kill you with just one bite or squeeze. To this end I will not include many details of this part of the trip, only to express a few major differences to being in SE Asia.

I have already mentioned the behaviour and demands of the children on the pier and the coldness of the rain but other things struck me as well. I became aware of the girth of most of the Australian people, these people were large and I appreciated feeling a normal size again. I was no longer an elephant in the land of the tiny people. The Australians have a knack of making people feel at home with their friendly, chilled, laid back approach to life. From the men in the bar who ask where I am from to the jogger who stopped in Brisbane to ask if I am lost. Lovely people. Just an observation, I did not see any mobility scooters in Asia, As soon as I landed in Australia there they were!

After exploring the east coast up to Fraser Island and back to Sydney I set off to explore a second Australian city, Melbourne. Melbourne was a relaxed end to my time away. It's a very chilled and young city. Apart from the weather, it felt very much like London or Oxford to me, very easy to navigate, lots of small, independent shops and wine bars. It had a real vibe about it. I went on a wine tour, surely an obligation whilst visiting Australia, and explored the very beautiful and dramatic Great Ocean Road.

It was my last opportunity for a gap before returning home from Sydney. I sat, enjoyed coffee, cheese and biscuits, wine, olives, all the pleasures of home but in the sunshine. I contemplated and reflected. I would be returning home in a week. I knew for certain that I could not aimlessly carry on the way I had been, enjoying the comfort of hotels and having little to do but watch and think. But I was determined not to waste the time feeling nostalgic or regretful that my time was almost up. I realized that I did not regret taking the decision to leave home and travel, not for a moment had I felt homesick. I had missed various people but any feelings of being apart had ben minimized by the social networks of Facebook and WhatsApp. We do live in a very small and beautiful world.

Home

Every dream has to come to an end, I knew that. As the time drew near to pack up and return home I felt calm. I was ready to return and I began thinking of my son who was to meet me at the airport the next morning. I began to plan meetings with friends and schedules to get necessary end of year accounts finalised for the business. I began to focus on going home.

I dreaded my time being over, my year of freedom, my year in flip-flops. Funnily enough the thought of having to put my feet back in to shoes filled me with dread. (On returning to work the tops of my toes, especially the little ones, became painful as blisters developed.) I thought about my return. As friends and family got in contact to make arrangements to meet or collect me from the airport I began to focus on what I was looking forward to on my return. I had missed my friends terribly, missing the pure joy of a simple chat. I had no regret of taking this decision to leave for a year and now I had to complete the journey by making the best of the return. I got in touch with friends and began to make arrangements where and when to meet up. This proved a positive approach.

The first hurdle to cross was the long flight home. I had ended up on the other side of the world! The trip from Australia back to the UK was a twenty-four hour flight, done with a short break of an hour in Singapore airport.

I decided to make the journey the best I possibly could. I knew I would be wedged in a seat and not able to get up or move about. I decided to view the entire journey as being a great opportunity of limitless films, wine, meals, coffee, listening to audio books, doing a bit of knitting if I could, reading, just simply making a real effort to focus on doing things I like and to forget about the length of the journey. I made myself a list of things I liked to do whilst travelling.

This worked really well. The plane was packed, I knew I wouldn't sleep but I made the best of it. I was right about being wedged in and had to wait a long time to visit the toilet whilst the passengers beside me slept through the night – lucky them!

At the first sight of UK soil my eyes filled up and became overwhelmed by a sense of joy. This was home, this was where I belonged and I was very pleased to see it again. My son met me at the airport and it was fantastic to see him. He had driven from Cardiff to Heathrow the night before, booked into a hotel close by, caught the bus to the airport after parking the car for twenty-four hours, and kept his room available for me to have a shower. That was welcome as well. The fact that he had achieved all of this by himself filled me with a sense of wonder and pride. This was a sign that my departure had brought about a time of maturity for him and I was glad. The fact that he had not yet got in the forces was another hurdle to be sorted out fairly shortly.

Air travel left me tired and dishevelled, but this was easily put right by a shower and a hair wash. We made our way back down the M4. Everything looked small and it was cold. Jet lag took over and I had a quick snooze in the car. It felt very odd being in one place yesterday the other side of the world, and being home today. Time felt as if it had passed in a flash now although, whilst I was away, the time appeared to go slowly. Being back in work I had the same strange sensation – had I really been gone a year or in fact been anywhere? It was the most surreal feeling.

The reaction of people to my return differed from person to person. Life goes on and went on. In some cases friends had gotten used to being without me and the reception was lukewarm. Thankfully workmates put up welcome banners, made cards and gave me a lovely photo album. I guess that social media made it appear that I hadn't gone far really and maybe hadn't been away, just on a very long holiday. They had pressures of their own and I had to accept this. I had taken the decision to step out and in some cases my space had been filled. But this was a positive factor too because it allowed me the freedom to go.

Most friends were interested in me and made arrangements to meet up for lunch or coffee so that 'I could tell them all about it…!' but this again filled me with dismay, where could I start? Some wanted to know which had been the best country, the best time, the best food, the best experience or maybe something that had gone wrong or frightened me. I was totally overwhelmed with how to begin to answer their interest, which was part of the reason I set out to write a book such as this.

Most of it is in these pages, the best bits, the funny bits, the people, the food, the memories, most of it is written here. I kept a daily journal of where I stayed and travelled so I could go back and refer if I needed to but it is all still in my mind. I close my eyes and I can be on a beach watching the sunset, or gazing in wonder at the temples in Bagan, or boarding a train, boat, bus… the smells, sounds, sights will remain with me. I will never regret the time I took to take my feet out of everyday shoes and place them in flip-flops – what a journey both in time and as a person.

Thank You – Thank You For Many Small Things And The Big Ones Too!

This trip had been something that I wanted for myself. It was conceived inside of me. I'm not sure where the desire or idea came from but I have never felt more certain that I was doing something at the right time and for me. Being a single mum I know that there are others who will agree with me that it can be difficult to do something completely for yourself after suppressing personal wishes for so long. I admit I struggled a bit with this concept but obviously not enough not to do it.

I remember being tearful when my son left from Singapore airport to return home after a visit but at no time did I cry or feel homesick. I felt bad about this but this is the truth. I recall lying in a hot, sweaty, noisy, dirty dormitory in Cambodia, whirling fan above my head and thinking about my lovely house in Cardiff, with my lovely bedroom and, most of all, my lovely roll top bath. I missed the luxury of my home but never for once regretted being away.

I thoroughly enjoyed my year away, travelling, teaching and living in a rural Thai village. I left with the promise to myself that if I didn't like it or I was uncomfortable, unsafe or ill at any time I was just a day's travel away from the safety and security of my home.

I have so much to be thankful for and so many people to thank for their participation and support during this year. It goes without saying that I am incredibly grateful to family members who have been around to support, watch out for and feed my children, who, by the way, are now young adults. But it was reassuring that family members were around for them. Social networks made it easy to remain in contact with friends with whom I would have normally met up on a regular basis for coffee, wine or meals but, as I have previously lamented, I did miss a good chat!

In addition, these networks provided other means of support and encouragement from other acquaintances, who remarked on photos and status through the year. So in a way I never did feel that far away even though I was. Using Facebook I was able to keep up on the lives of friends and email others for more lengthy updates or sometimes just a splurge from me! For this constant support of family and friends I am grateful. Thank you.

I am grateful for the time that I was able to take away from the business, being supported by an excellent work team who carried on without me. I did wonder at times if I was even missed but this was what I wanted, what I planned for. I didn't want my choice to cause any more work or hassle for anyone. I am thankful that I had the resources to book the flights, take the necessary health precautions and have enough money to start me off. Having said this, once in SE Asia everything is so cheap, cheap to travel, stay in hostels, eat and drink (as long as you stick to beer...). It cost me less to be away. My house rent paid my mortgage.

But what I am really grateful for was the kindness of strangers and fellow travellers. I have learnt to become an observer of the small things in life and the beauty in the small acts of others. I learnt to appreciate.

From the lady with her hot coffee in plastic cups on plastic stools at four a.m. in Hanoi after a night's train travel, to being helped to cross busy junctions in Saigon, to the smiles of strangers when I sat alone on buses, trains, boats or dinner tables. For the people who have approached me in airports, bus or train stations to enquire as to where I needed to go or what I was looking for and then showing me the way. For the gentleman who carried my rucksack from the boat at Railay after we were dropped off in the sea. For the twelve-year-old boy who gave me a lift on his motorbike up the long jetty to the taxi rank in Krabi (Yes, he really was twelve!) and for the tuk tuk driver who carried my bag up the steps in the hostel in Kohn Kaen.

So many small acts of kindness but for each one I am totally overwhelmed with gratitude. Added to this endless list could be the group of ladies on the Mekong Delta who shared laughter and food with me, gave up and cleaned seats for me to sit down, or the taxi driver who insisted I meet his wife and children in Kuala Lumpur to eat with them... the list of these nameless people is long.

I have never felt alone or frightened. I have felt welcome and content in their countries and in their company. People smiled at me all the time. This was in sharp contrast to my experience in the UK of being middle-aged and invisible.

Thank you for the food! So many different things I have tried, some never to try again but each was an experience. It was interesting how different our palates are. The Asians favour hot, spicy, sweet food, whereas I would prefer the salty, creamy, meaty tastes of our cuisine. Marmite was not appreciated, neither was blue cheese or even sprouts. But I in return could not stomach their barra, a pot of rotten, fermented fish. And for any Australians reading this, Vegemite will never make up for Marmite. Thank you for the variety of drinks: rice wine, rice wine with tarantulas floating in the bottom of the bottle, the tea, the beer and, of course, the wine. Thank you.

I have learnt so much this year. One thing was certain though – always grab the window seat. I always make straight for a window seat whatever I am travelling in or on. I fail to understand people who travel with the blinds down and sleep the whole journey. Surely it's all about the journey? Smile, always smile and ask politely if you need something or a direction. Taste everything that is offered but say if you don't like it. Accept kindness and hospitality, and return the favour if possible.

For my final evening I booked myself in to the Shangri La Hotel in Sydney, just a short walk away from Circular Quay and the Rocks. I struggled up the many steps from the quay after getting off the Manly Ferry, my rucksack heavy on my back, looking hot and bothered from my climb as I joined the other guests waiting to check in. I felt really out of place, like I should have been booking into a hostel somewhere else. The hotel staff were polite and efficient, I didn't feel out of place for long. But the most amazing thing happened, I got upgraded to a suite. I was so amazed and thankful I stood and cried in the room. What better finish could I have asked for? Perfect, and it had a large, whirlpool bath. I had struggled to justify paying so much for a room for myself but this was the icing on the cake, a kind of permission granted and I was so grateful. It was time to head home.